T0208378

IT'S ALL GOOD

How to Create Your Life on Purpose ...
Rather Than Playing Victim to It

An Autobiographical Text/Self-Improvement Book

Pamela Poli DiSarro

BALBOA.
PRESS

A DIVISION OF HAY HOUSE

Balboa Press books may be ordered through booksellers or by contacting:

Balboa Press
A Division of Hay House
1663 Liberty Drive
Bloomington, IN 47403
www.balboapress.com
1 (877) 407-4847

Because of the dynamic nature of the Internet, any web addresses or links contained in this book may have changed since publication and may no longer be valid. The views expressed in this work are solely those of the author and do not necessarily reflect the views of the publisher, and the publisher hereby disclaims any responsibility for them.

The author of this book does not dispense medical advice or prescribe the use of any technique as a form of treatment for physical, emotional, or medical problems without the advice of a physician, either directly or indirectly. The intent of the author is only to offer information of a general nature to help you in your quest for emotional and spiritual well-being. In the event you use any of the information in this book for yourself, which is your constitutional right, the author and the publisher assume no responsibility for your actions.

Any people depicted in stock imagery provided by Getty Images are models, and such images are being used for illustrative purposes only. Certain stock imagery © Getty Images.

Print information available on the last page.

ISBN: 978-1-9822-3419-5 (sc)
ISBN: 978-1-9822-3420-1 (e)

Balboa Press rev. date: 09/26/2019

Contents

Introduction

On the lovely spring day of June 7, 1952, the bucolic scene was set in the small town of Chestnut Hill, Massachusetts, outside Boston. Edmund Leon Poli Jr. was dressed in cap and gown and dizzy with excitement as he lined up for his graduation from prestigious Boston College. He was surrounded by family, all except for his lovely wife, Rosemary, who had just been taken to the hospital that morning to deliver their first child. I was born at 9:30 AM that symbolic day.

Fast-forward thirty-plus years. I was traveling the country with some of the greatest metaphysical minds of the twentieth century. This one day, while I was at a retreat, Dr. Larry Jensen, a pioneer in the human potential movement, guided a group of students I was a part of through a Kundalini meditation. He was regressing us as far back in our lives as we could go to expose us to our own way of mastery. I very distinctly remember this darkness overcame me, and then, a sudden pressure burst forth, as if I were being birthed. The sense of terror was beyond anything I'd ever experienced before. I screamed and woke myself from this almost trancelike state. Regaining consciousness, I then went to my room to telephone my mother and tell her of my experience. Hearing it, she was shocked and proceeded to tell me the story of her terrifying pregnancy and the birth of yours truly, Pamela Jane Poli.

When my mother, Rosemary, was almost two years old, she became very ill. She was taken to a local Boston hospital, where doctors discovered her appendix had ruptured and peritonitis had set in. Her life hung in the balance. They operated, and she survived, but my grandmother was told that her daughter would never have children. What a surprising insight I had realized through Kundalini meditation; I was born in fear.

My parents came from two very different socioeconomic backgrounds, born and raised in the puritanical yet cosmopolitan city of Boston. My father was from an aristocratic Italian family that lived in the affluent suburb of Brookline. My mother came from a lower-middle-class German, Austrian, and Irish family from South Boston. Compared to today's stats, they were young to be married and raising a family. But two children raising children wasn't odd in the 1950s. My mother was an only child and genuinely wanted a large family, so after the surprising outcome of her first pregnancy, she daringly had four more children.

I'm reluctant to use the term *dysfunctional*, as I believe it is the most overused term of the twentieth century, but, oh yes, a lot of dysfunction went on in our household and in our extended family. My father's mother, my Nonna, was not happy about my parents' union. Nonna was an educated woman who graduated from Jackson College (which later became Radcliffe College). She spoke three languages—English, Italian, and French—and was quite a snob. I think she thought my father married below his status. She had contempt for my mother, which was extremely evident and made holidays with family a challenge. I am still, however, of the conviction that most Italians are easygoing; my dad was a really comical guy. Mom was more responsible, with a tad of stubborn Germanic stock mixed in, so they butted heads quite a bit. Dad did adore Mom and had a hard time paying attention to us kids, as she was all he had eyes for, so to speak.

My mom was a beauty and a great homemaker. She used to take us kids to antique shops and pick up affordable pieces of furniture for the house. She loved to refinish them and even painted on canvas and drew pictures for our school for the holidays. Dad wanted nothing more than to see my mother happy. I don't think he was really honest with her about finances, as they seemed to struggle with them at times. The *lack consciousness* we read about in today's self-help literature was the foundation of much of the upset in our daily lives. We had not enough time, not enough love, not enough money, and the list goes on and on.

My introduction to spirituality came at a very young age. My best friend, Rosie, lived on top of what I thought was a mountain, right across the street from my house. When I was around seven or eight, and old enough to go to Rosie's on my own, I would make my way "up the mountain" on the path I forge to play games outside and would run and jump from rock to rock on the ledge that made up her yard. We almost never went into the house to play because Rosie's mother was very sick. She mostly rested in her bedroom all day. Rosie's father seemed a bit older than most dads and was rarely there when I was. He was very quiet but kind when he did speak to us. The house was eerily still and lightless, except for the many candles lit in front of a picture of the Sacred Heart of Jesus.

One day, I ran up the hill to her house and knocked at the door, but no one was home. I remember thinking someone was usually always at her house, but I let it go. When I returned the next day, lots of cars were in the driveway, and the house sounded busy—something I'd never heard before at Rosie's house. I don't remember how I found out, but I discovered Rosie's mother had died. It was the first time I had known anyone who passed away. I didn't know what to think or feel, and I didn't see my friend that day. Somehow, I just knew that when she was ready, she would come find me. Sure enough, a week later, we got together to play. She never mentioned what had happened, and I didn't ask questions.

I do have a vivid memory of the day when one of Rosie's sisters confessed to Rosie and I she had seen her mother's spirit at the foot of her bed in the middle of the night. She told us that it woke her up and appeared as a bright light with a shadow of her image and a smile on her face. Rosie's little sister wasn't afraid, and she was younger than us, so we decided not to be afraid either. Many occasions after that, Rosie and her sisters believed they felt and saw their mother's celestial being. I wondered if this happened to everyone who lost a loved one, but I never discussed it with another person. It didn't unnerve me, and part of me wished I could see this vision and hoped one day I would.

One Sunday evening Rosie came to my house to watch the movie "Our Lady of Fatima." It's a parable about the legend of the apparition of the Virgin Mary, appearing before a group of children in the town of Fatima, Portugal. We just loved the story and made a game of it by creating a quiet place on the ledge of rocks surrounded by trees in my friends' yard, where we would pray and wait for the vision to be shown to us. I still have memories of those peaceful times with nature where I felt pure joy and jubilation. There was a sense of serenity and safety as we lost ourselves in our imagination. Eventually we moved and Rosie faded out of my life, but she was never forgotten.

The 1960's and the 1970's seemed to be a time of cultural transformation as it was the advent of the New Age movement or the Age of Aquarius. People were resolutely voicing a need for change. Within the coalition of this era there was a vibration that was attracting something bigger than the eye could see.

The Woodstock Music and Arts Festival took place in Upstate New York the summer before my senior year in high school. It made a tremendous impact on my generation and was a pivotal event in pop-culture and music history. Times, oh yes, they were a-changing, as the song so plainly says. The Kent State shootings erupted a few weeks before my high school graduation. On May 4, 1970, the Ohio National Guard fired into a crowd of students demonstrating at Kent State University, killing four and wounding nine students. A nationwide student strike took place, which symbolized the profound legislative and social chasm that divided the country during the Vietnam War era. The political climate was contentious and very pertinent to the youth of humanity I was part of.

During this time, a well-known Harvard psychologist, Timothy Leary, advocated the use of psychedelic drugs and wrote about his drug experiences. People were using marijuana and hallucinogenic drugs recreationally to expand their consciousness. Many followed this new-age culture. The Beatles and other artists created music that brought to light truths no one beyond the ancient philosophers had explored. Most baby boomers can reminisce about our bell-bottom jeans and tie-dyed T-shirts. The nomenclature of a person of this ideology went from *beatnik* to *hippie*. At the time, I felt proud to be one. I read hundreds of books by brilliant holistic authors, including Carlos Castaneda, who was an American author with a PhD in anthropology. He wrote a series of books that illustrate his training in shamanism, particularly with a group from Mexico called the Toltecs. I especially enjoyed *The Teachings of Don Juan* and *A Separate Reality*. I will expand on that reality in the pages that follow, but the point is studies of that era were acknowledging that another consciousness lay beyond thought and feeling. In fact, in quantum mechanics, we have discovered that the entire Universe is a series of possibilities.

College was a blur, a mix of soft drugs and alcohol. I was submersed in the Midwest at the Jesuit university Marquette. As an East Coast girl, getting tossed into Milwaukee, Wisconsin, was really far from a good fit. I functioned pretty well nonetheless, as my guilt-ridden "mainframe" kept me under control and in check. Soon enough, I realized that I was at the wrong university for the wrong reason. Enrolling in a four-year program for dental hygiene had seemed reasonable at the time. I had chosen this course of study believing that I would have a stable job when I graduated. I never wanted to worry about employment or money. At that time, hygienists made excellent salaries, and the four-year degree would also allow me to teach. Suffice it to say, my parents really couldn't afford this school, and I had never really considered what my passions were when I chose this path.

After a year and a half of personal emotional confusion mixed with my family's financial turmoil, I decided to leave Marquette and go back east. As drama had always been the dictum of my life, I dramatically changed course and questioned who, what, where, and why. My answers to these questions were pretty esoteric, and I began to examine the purpose of my life and what I genuinely wanted to do with it. The desire and the need to feel connected became my mission. I committed myself to a syllabus of psychology and philosophy along with metaphysics, and mixed these sciences with the desire and the intuitive need to be creative. I had always loved the arts as a child and found enjoyment and satisfaction in drawing and creating decoupages and collages. Concentrating on my predilections, I enrolled in art school and studied *interior design* and architecture (never really seeing the double meaning of *interior design* until almost three decades later). Having refocused on my interior life and my creative inclinations, I found the shifts in my awareness made a difference in all facets of who I was. Learning was, and still is, my deepest desire, and I never stopped studying. My wish to become more aligned and my desire to live more mindfully took me on a journey beyond my wildest dreams.

When I was twenty-two, my boyfriend, Alan, and I decided to get married. Convinced that it was the mature, safe, and adult thing to do, we planned a wedding. Shortly thereafter, I managed to get a lucky break and find apprentice work in a well-known Boston design studio. I was the assistant or "girl Friday" to four interior designers. The experience was invaluable to my dream to create my own business one day. My husband worked for his father in a family-owned automobile dealership on the North Shore of Boston. Life was pretty ideal—that is, until it wasn't. I became disillusioned as a young married woman, as my spouse worked nights and weekends. He, too, was unhappy with his demanding work schedule and his absent home life, as we were two ships passing in the night. I started thinking about our choices and opportunities. I felt that we were young enough that, before we started a family, an excursion through Europe would be a valuable experience. I had always yearned to go to Italy and meet some family I still had there. So, we planned our sabbatical. But this holiday had no return ticket. We sold our cars, put our furniture in storage, and went off on Christmas Day in 1975.

First, we visited friends in Paris and traveled through France, enjoying the French and relishing their culture. Soon enough, though, I itched for the trip through the country that was calling my name. We bought rail passes and stayed in pensions all over northern Italy. The excitement was palpable as we enthusiastically toured museums and basilicas daily. We visited my cousins in Lucca and had Sunday dinner at my uncle Americo's house. That very evening, we went for a promenade through the piazza, as was apparently the custom in this captivating little village. This simple passage created memories for me steeped in camaraderie and sentiment.

We left my family to continue our journey and visit the major cities of this country. It just so happened that two of our closest friends, and my painting instructors, Rita and Bud Guzzi, had advised us to visit Positano, on the Amalfi Coast. As it says in the travel guide, "It is the coast's most picturesque and photogenic town, with steeply stacked houses tumbling down to the sea in a cascade of sun-bleached peach, pink and terracotta colors." Let me tell you, it is all of that and then some. Our actual plan was to go to Positano and then go straight across to Bari on the opposite coast of the peninsula. From there, we planned to take the ferry to Greece. Well, I'm sure you'll never guess. We fell in love with Italy and didn't leave Positano for nearly two years.

We made friends with the locals and various artists who lived there. We found jobs and lived in a quaint one-room studio up at the top of this mountain village. Our tiny glass homestead that overlooked the majestic bay was owned by singer-songwriter Shawn Phillips, who lived in Positano for most of the 1970s. He and his family became our good friends. They, along with a group of comrades from town, helped us learn the language by declining verbs on napkins at the local cafés, mornings and evenings. We were genuinely living a remarkable chronicle of fortuity, or was it really? Was it random good fortune, or did things happen because of certain laws of nature? These laws we seem to naturally take for granted. As I look back, I can clearly see how they were working precisely as they were meant to. In the chapters that follow, I will outline the seven laws of nature and guide you on how orderly and deliberately the Universe functions. For now, I just want to share this halcyon existence I experienced.

At the end of a wonderful summer in this tropical paradise, I began to experience a feeling of excitement and an intuitive knowing that I was going to have my first child. I went for an examination, and sure enough, it confirmed the news of our pending parenthood. I wanted to have my baby back in America, so we planned our return in the fall of that year. My beautiful daughter Colby was born on the first day of spring, March 20, 1978. Until that memorable day, I had thought I knew what love was. But it felt as if my heart would explode when my precious little seven-pound baby girl was placed in my arms. What a splendid blessing life had bestowed on me from our cherished time abroad.

Shortly after our return to the United States and the birth of my daughter, my marriage began to fall apart. My husband just didn't want to work, nor did he feel he could take care of our daughter. Working with a partner, I started to build an interior design business while my husband stayed home, trying to decide what he wanted to do with his life. Our daughter was in day care two or three days a week because we couldn't afford any more than that. It became difficult to pay the rent and stay afloat with my new business as our only income. The financial and emotional pressure strained our relationship, and we separated. *How is this happening to us?* I thought. Something had to change insomuch as our marriage was deteriorating. Colby was a little over a year old when we got a divorce. I will not even pretend that life was easy alone, working and raising my baby girl. I really think the fall from such a utopian couple of years to a life of mechanical routine and day-to-day toil traumatized me. The breakup left me distressed, but my love for my daughter kept me smiling and fed my soul. I was frightened but not disheartened.

One evening, my business partner invited me to a political party. It was a party to support a candidate for Boston mayor. I didn't go out very often but decided that a night out would be good for me. As fate would have it, I met a man, Steven DiSarro, who was a metropolitan developer, and we chatted about real estate and design. A few weeks later, he called me and asked for consultation on a project he was undertaking in the Back Bay of Boston. We got the job and many more after that. Eventually, our relationship became more than a working one. We courted for two years and were married at a magnificent home in Newton he bought for us. It was a decorator's dream house. The day he took me to see it, we had our tour, and then excused ourselves to discuss the property outside. He asked me if I liked it, and of course, I said it was wonderful. He then grasped my hand and took me back inside, where we informed the agent that we wanted to buy the house and would have papers signed the next day. It was like a fairy tale, and I didn't really sleep that night because I was so overwhelmed with surprise and joy.

Steven, too, had been married before and had a daughter, Kim. She was just two years older than my daughter Colby, and it all seemed to fit so well. Still in my twenties, I was determined to have the family I always imagined and wanted. Being in love and excited about building a family together, we recognized the blessing of a second chance.

Our life was itself full of ambitions and determination. I ran my business part-time and also collaborated with my husband, who was assiduous about his work. Not long after my first son Steven Jr. was born, my husband came to me and asked if I would be opposed to him opening a nightclub. This didn't surprise me, as his closest friend and best man at our wedding was the largest club owner in the city of Boston. I blessed his venture, designed the interior with the architect, and helped him build the business. Club Soda was actualized and became a commercial success. Eventually, we constructed another club in Pompano, Florida, near a home we built in Boca Raton. Things were exciting and provocative at the same time. Three little boys, Steven Jr., Nicholas, and Michael, were born in the blink of an eye. We traveled back and forth quite a bit because the children were young enough that school wasn't really an issue. We were in Florida Thursday to Monday most weeks in the winter, and the children loved it.

For me and my fast-growing family's circumstances changed dramatically in a very short period of time. It seems destiny had a different idea than I did for the way things would play out. Lady Luck appeared to abandon our ménage, and loss came in multiples. The real-estate business crashed in the late 1980s, and that stress put pressure on us across the board, as we suffered considerable financial losses. I and the children rarely saw my husband, as he worked days at one job and nights at the other. We did seem to have a glimmer of hope when Steven had the opportunity to acquire a large apartment complex for conversion. He was one of the first condominium developers in Boston and had a natural talent for real estate. As fate would have it, the funding came through my ex-father-in-law, who was on the board of directors of a Boston bank. He knew my husband and had admired his expertise. We were confident and enthusiastic as we pressed on.

On Christmas Eve that fateful year, our family and friends were coming for our traditional holiday dinner party. Steven came home early that evening, and as we were preparing for our guests, he put on the television to watch the news. There we saw it, the apartment building that he had just contracted was on fire and on the national news channels because it was Christmas Eve. It seemed someone in one of the units had been barbecuing on their balcony and the wind blew over their hibachi. The draperies in the apartment caught fire, and the fire quickly spread. No one was hurt, but many were displaced, and because of the wind and weather, the building was all but destroyed. My husband did have insurance, of course, but this delayed development much longer than expected.

In the midst of all of this, I lost my father, a stunning heartbreak. He was divorced from my mother, alone and suffering from heart disease. We became very close at the end of his life, something I had always wanted but that had seemed elusive. No matter how ill a parent is or how prepared you think you are, you are never really ready to lose a father or a mother. I experienced crushing pain and sadness when he died, and it took me quite a while to recover. I remember asking a dear friend of mine why this heartbreak was filling me with such a deluge of emotion. She suggested that I see it as if my father had given me an opportunity to grieve for a lifetime of unresolved heartache. *A silver lining,* I thought. What a fascinating viewpoint. I appreciated the freedom to acknowledge and let go of all the sadness I had hidden away for so long.

Our marriage suffered through this arduous time, and things got rather ugly. Steven was never home. We rarely if ever communicated, and when he was there, we would continually argue. He would tell me that I was a conundrum to him and that our discussions had no gray areas, just black and white. Not an easy comment to decipher, especially for an artist and designer. Our arguments got more and more inexhaustible. Wanting to be a good wife and support my husband through this challenging time, I did the best I could to accept life's fortuitousness.

We had lost our home and cars and were going through corporate and personal bankruptcy. It's not uncommon for a man—especially a man as successful as my husband—to become depressed and angry when faced with financial loss. Who better to take your anger out on than the person closest to you? The intensity of his verbal attacks eventually began to worry me, and one morning, after an uncomfortable and shocking exchange of words, I realized that this was not what I wanted my children to witness.

We were extremely fortunate that our two girls were closer than most biological sisters. It so pleased me that they confided in each other as they did. They were happy as a family with their brothers and seemed balanced and well adjusted. For that reason, we reluctantly **se**parated, and the children and I moved into a house my mother owned and was about to sell, as she had just remarried. We left our palatial thirteen-room home in Newton and moved to a seven-room Cape Cod style home in the country town of Westwood. I painted and cleaned and moved our paraphernalia in, going back and forth for weeks. There I was, with my two youngest in car seats, each day filling my beat-up old Jeep Wagoneer, which I had bought with $5,000 my father had left me after his passing. It was all I had, but I was glad I had it. My brother-in-law and a friend moved some furniture for us when the house was ready.

Having grown up in a home with a whole lot of contention and discourse, I had a deep fear of quarreling. I had never learned what to do with this discomfort, so denial or avoidance was my answer. The experience of separating, moving, and raising the children on my own was very disconcerting. My temperament and feelings ran up and down the emotional scale—fear, resentment, frustration. Another failed relationship, and I perceived myself as hopeless, incapable, and defeated. I had to do everything alone, which caused me to feel isolated and detached. Eventually, I sought help from a therapist, and I used these troublesome, discomforting emotions in an affirming way, rather than avoiding or fearing them. They actually gave me the energy to get it all done. This didn't resemble what I had planned for us all; nevertheless, I was fortunate to have my family and the home they gave to us.

I remember being worried sick about how I would provide for my household. My youngest child wasn't even of school age, and the last two boys were only fourteen months apart. For a long time, there were two cribs, two high chairs, and two car seats, and my older son, Steven Jr., wasn't even five years old. At one point, I had to waitress at a restaurant close to our home just to put food on the table and have cash in my hand. I recall writing prayers on index cards at times and completely immersing myself in my spiritual reading and metaphysical investigation. I did my design work on a much smaller scale, when I could. Our lives had changed dramatically, and still, we were all safe and seemingly unbroken, holding it together.

After a little over a year of this, when things started to shift again, my husband and I considered a reconciliation. The year of separation had seemed to have changed him, or so I desperately wanted to believe. He spent more time with me and the children than ever before. For the first time in our fifteen-year relationship, thirteen of those years married, things were open to discussion, and he humbly revealed his vulnerability. Soon enough, we agreed he would move into our little house. He found time to coach the boys' sports teams and be home for dinner, something that had very rarely happened before. We had very little in terms of financial security, compared to our impressive past, but I'm probably more grateful for this short season than any other period in the years gone by.

The day after Mother's Day, May 10, 1993, was the last time I ever saw my husband. We had an argument on Mother's Day because I had to travel for a project I was doing and he was very adamant about me not going. He left the house that morning without saying goodbye, and that surprised me, so I looked out the window when he left. I saw him get into a car I did not recognize. I never saw him again; he just disappeared. Suffice it to say, the bottom of my world fell right out. I didn't know what to think, how to feel, or what to do. I didn't even go to the police for two weeks because I was afraid that he had reverted back to his old behaviors and was punishing me for the argument. The day after I reported him missing, my name appeared on the front page of the Boston *Herald* newspaper with a two-page story about him, his business, and his questionable associations with some people I'd never heard of. People made all sorts of assumptions, and I feared for what my older children would hear and have to deal with. I kept a strong front and attempted to support the family while dealing with the queries about their father's sudden departure. After a while, I knew in my heart he had died, because his voluntary abandonment just didn't ring true to me.

Over the next decade, I felt extremely alone and had to endure situations that I had never dreamed would be part of my life. For example, I had to deal with the IRS. Since there was no body to declare him deceased, the IRS came after me for back taxes in exorbitant amounts. The FBI were regularly coming to our home and asking questions.

Soon enough, I discovered Steven had made acquisitions in my name, so in the end, I had to file for personal bankruptcy for almost a million dollars. A friend of mine owned a bartering service, so I bartered my design services to employ an attorney. I even had to testify in front of the grand jury, never losing faith, though, and trusting and affirming that we would get through this. Eventually, I was able to find steady, rewarding, full-time employment in management within the design field, with an income to nominally support my family. Nights and weekends, I was determined to do independent interior design work, when feasible, to fill the financial voids of raising my large family.

Upward and onward was my game plan, and I tried not to fumble. I was extremely motivated, searching for the answers to this story I called my life. My family's need for a competent, productive parent gave me the impetus to hold on to the lifelines available.

Ultimately, I decided to literally entrust myself to the study of metaphysics, attending innumerable seminars and workshops. The children were my main preoccupation, and I could see that the distress of this heartache was wearing on them, especially the boys. After what seemed like an instant, I had four teenagers and a stepdaughter, who was distant, to say the least. She was now living with her mother full-time, and we rarely saw her. The transition was huge for all of them, and cracks started to appear within the family unit.

The three boys started exhibiting rebellious behaviors, which I felt ill equipped to deal with. They were defiant and unruly and acted out, leaving me fearful and angry. My adolescent daughter Colby was overseeing the home front after school, a job the boys made arduous. They were hard on me when I would set limits, challenging everything I asked of them. God knows I prayed and did whatever I could to create a stable environment. Eventually, I hired a male babysitter, a retired serviceman, to be at my home after school and take some pressure off Colby. The boys liked him, and it worked until he needed more free time and gave me his notice.

My brother-in-law even took the boys to the Scared Straight program he had heard about at the courthouse, where he was working as a clerk. Everyone did their best to help in this very disconcerting situation. I'm sure the children were angry about what looked like abandonment by their father. It was harder to see the effects this suspicious decampment had on the girls. They seemed to hide their pain in less obvious ways. That's not to say they didn't experience the psychological trauma of such a dreadful loss. They all went to counseling, but no one can force a child to talk or listen. The lack of closure was taking its toll on each of my children. It was, to say the least, a very challenging parenthesis for all.

It wasn't long before I began to see that I had deluded myself into believing that I was okay. "What we resist persists" is a truth that was revealed to me so very clearly on September 11, 2001. The day after the devastating disaster, I was driving my car through town when I heard a radio announcer commenting on how sad it was for the families of the victims of September 11. He went on to say how all those mothers', fathers', sisters', and brothers' lives were changed forever in an instant. I immediately felt a sorrow so profound that I cried for almost two weeks. I finally felt safe in my sorrow and tears as a nation was in mourning for so many souls and a freedom that was forever compromised because of that infamous day. I realized that I hadn't given myself the gift of bereavement when my husband disappeared and our family dynamic changed forever—*dynamic* being the operative term, which I use to describe the force that affected my children's development and stability. Believing that they needed me to mirror strength and safety, I blocked my energy and my feelings as I had through all the most formidable experiences in my life.

On the tenth anniversary of my husband's disappearance, I held a memorial Mass for Steven DiSarro Sr. I published the date, time, and location in our local newspaper and invited family and friends. Everyone came to my house after the Mass. I scattered enlarged and framed photos of Steven Sr. and the children throughout the house. We had coffee and pastries and spoke about Steve as we all observed the pictures of baptisms and birthdays and made his absence real. I planned this tribute because I wanted my children to have the closure and the respect for their loss that most families receive when a loved one passes. Most of my husband's business associates and colleagues came, and it really was an epilogue for our family.

It took twelve years to hear the truth of his death. The police notified me that they finally had information for me. Frank Salemme, the New England mob boss had admitted to having knowledge of the crime in an attempt to lessen his time incarcerated as part of a plea bargain. It seems that just before his alleged desertion, my husband and his various partners had been building another nightclub at the Four Point Channel in Boston. It just so happened that one day some FBI agents came to see him at the construction site. Steve had grown up on Federal Hill in providence Rhode Island and was known to have familiarity with some underworld personalities. He rarely discussed any of this with me and call me naive; I never wanted to know. I can only postulate that someone saw my husband with these FBI agents and questioned what Steve could, would or did say to them, which made someone fearful enough to take his life.

In order to genuinely expand on this passage, we call life, it became necessary for me to confront the zealot who still lay dormant within. Addiction, whether to drugs, alcohol, food, or whatever, is a formidable disease, cunning, baffling, and insidious. The tough part is that it disguises itself and enslaves the victim. I was confronted by my sons at one point and by my brothers and sisters at another time to examine my wine drinking every evening. I had to decide to get vigorously honest, or at least be willing to. *Disease*, the operative word, is just what it says—uneasiness, or not being at ease. In hindsight, I thought I had quelled a lot of the fear within, but was I really comfortable and at peace with my life? Thank goodness I had a place to go and delve even deeper into the shadows of the past. I had explored AA meetings and fellowship when my youngest son was born and my life and marriage had become unmanageable. Again, it was time to trust life and question my continence. Within the camaraderie of meetings, I found a common ground I had only yearned for. I vigorously filled my life with sobriety and did the twelve steps, which supported the essential changes to shift this precedent.

Life got better, and I again became lighthearted as I enthusiastically began to empower myself. Finances were limited, but I enlisted the help of a life coach, Laura Fredrickson, to work with me privately. We worked together once a week for quite a few years, which naturally transformed the way I saw things and felt. She taught me to take personal responsibility for creating my life through choice and conscious awareness. I relished the support this provided and the plethora of metaphysical knowledge she made clear within our hour sessions. I appreciated the shifts in my perception and the freedom of unlimited potential. I began to change the way I looked at thing and the things I looked at changed, as Wayne Dyer so brilliantly affirmed. My studies grew deeper and more intimate than ever before.

Laura and I spoke remotely by phone, as she was on the West Coast and I was on the East Coast. Our calls were so extensive I recorded each one and would play them back over and over. She truly inspired me, and I suddenly became open to the possibility of a career change. Life coaching was something I absolutely wanted to explore and expand on. After extensive course study, I received my certification. I then married my years of interior design and my life coaching and created REALeyes NOW, a business that guides people to be at home in their heart and create heart in their home. I love what I do and have not looked back. I trust that this is the mission and purpose for this girl's life. I feel it in my bones and sinews.

Finding any kind of peace surrounding our tragedy has been a long time coming for me and my family. To this day, the wounds of the past continually bring to light opportunities for healing. "Life is for healing," as it says in *A Course of Miracles*. What we do with our pain and how we utilize it will make the difference in our future life outcomes. I chose to use what I've learned and studied over the years and devote myself to educating and influencing the general public with the truth that goes beyond what appears to be real.

I've learned so much from some of my greatest challenges. I no longer use the term *problem* except with a definition, as "a question proposed for solution or discussion." My history is just that—over and done. Yes, it is part of me, but it cannot deplete or extinguish the light and love within. The ego tries to control us by using our attachment to the past. It capitalizes on our guilt and shame to keep us under its thumb. Empowerment is in the now, and forgiveness is always the answer. With the power of choice, I decided to learn and understand how we were created and what works in order to heal. I discovered that it was necessary to go deep within and bridge the gap between body and spirit. For a long time now, I have wanted to end the cycle of dysfunction and insanity for my family and claim my natural inheritance of pure love, a truth I believe with all my heart.

I intend to become the woman and spiritual guide I am meant to be. A knowing and a passion persist within me that this is and has always been my calling. Most times, while meditating, I can so very clearly see myself speaking to groups of people and sharing the truths of our authentic nature. At these times, I feel a connection that brings me true joy and exuberance.

We are all magnificent beyond description. Only our limited perspective keeps us small and disenfranchised. It is my hope and plan to navigate you downstream with the natural flow of life as we are meant to live it. Let the journey be a fluid course to the true reality of this infinitely giving and loving Universe, available to us all.

This book was always there for me to receive and pass on to you. It demonstrates that we are all one. It chronicles a journey, my story of awakening beyond the ego's limits to the authentic self or spirit within. It is my mission and purpose to guide people to their hearts and to assist them to find inspiration in life's circumstances. Our minds and hearts are partners in the experience of life. Our emotions are our natural GPS. If we can consciously function from a higher perspective and gain clarity and vision, we can become the deliberate creators we are meant to be.

When my young children (who are now blessed young adults) and I were distressed and overwhelmed by life's heartbreaks, my oldest son Steven would always say to me, "Don't worry Mom, It's all good." I didn't quite understand it then, as it seemed like a conundrum. I sure get it now, and know you will too, if you are willing to see things differently and open up to the miracles in the pages to follow.

1

Who Am I?

I understand you may feel dismayed that you are starting with such a profound question. Really, where am I going with this one? Well, I want to have you engaging in this thought process right out of the gate. Why? Because most likely, you don't believe that you are the powerful creator you are. You don't believe that your thoughts are anything or that your inner dialogue is keyed into energy or the laws of nature. Innately, however, you do know that there is something more to how and why things happen as they do in our lives. So why do you feel powerless? This feeling leaves you wanting answers to questions you're afraid to ask. Simon Sinek wrote an intriguing book titled *Start with Why*. He studied history's most influential leaders, and he discovered they all asked, "Why?" So now let me ask you this: Why do you feel so unfulfilled, so victimized, so stressed, and so overwhelmed when you have more opportunity and possibility than people have had at any other time in history? The twenty-first century is an evolutionary time for new-age holistic and spiritual consciousness-raising movements. Here's one for you: spiritual evolution has its own Facebook page. Social media, so prevalent in our society, can be a very useful tool to help shift our global expansion and assist in our understanding of who we are. So, let's seriously ask this very basic question and listen closely.

I suggest that you sit in silence, eyes closed, for a moment and really ask yourself and your inner guide this. The responses you get will amaze you, and the insights can truly lead you to a deeper understanding. Let me help you out, though, with a broader perception of a truth that was somehow overlooked in our emotional training, as we were living and maturing in our time-based reality, we call *life*. You are a divine Spirit in a human body. You are not just a body or an impartial person in the Universe. You are an integral part of the Universe. That's right, and the Universe in you is endless, eternal, deathless, and all-loving, and the essence of who you are. We are not separate from the Infinite Universal Intelligence that created us, just as a drop of ocean water is part of the ocean and can never be anything other than what it is. You are, in essence, a drop of the Universe and can never be anything other than that.

The first book I read that was analogous to my query of who we really are was *You Can Heal Your Life*, by author and motivational speaker Louise Hay. My mother signed and gave me this influential self-help handbook when I was in my late twenties. The writing was easy to read, made incredible sense, and answered my *why*. Louise Hay became the mother of the new-age movement, a consciousness-raising movement that really interested me; wrote many amazing books; and inspired many people to take responsibility for creating their own lives. She opened my eyes to the belief that we came into this physical reality from a nonphysical reality. Yes, we came into form on this planet, and we chose to come here to learn a particular lesson. And the ability to learn this lesson precedes our spiritual progress. We also have the volition to select our sex, our skin color, our homeland, and even our parents. They actually mirror the paradigms of what you came to work on in this lifetime.

The twenty-first century is an enlightening time in our evolution. People today don't want to just talk about miracles; they want to create them. What we are finding out is that we can actually do just that.

You are an extension of our Source energy, or nonphysical energy, even though you are in a physical form. Although you are a physical being on this planet and you have access to this broader perspective of nonphysical energy, your connection to the nonphysical Source may have sidetracked you. Most people forget this connection over time and cultivate a deep-rooted resistance to their natural connection to Universal Intelligence or the Source.

I intend to help you remember the truth of who you are and the miraculous power of the now. When you understand that there is nothing more valuable than *feeling good now*, you will have it all. The real purpose of your time here is to succeed, through life experience, in enjoying our natural inheritance of expansion, true joy, and freedom. Let's awaken the infinite powers that lay dormant inside that will return us to our innately loving and magnificent souls. With this understanding, you'll be able to perceive that "it's all good."

Background on *A Course in Miracles*

I am a student and a teacher of the metaphysical study called *A Course in Miracles* (ACIM). I feel it necessary to give a little bit of background on ACIM at this time, as so many people ask me, "What is this *course in miracles*?" As Wikipedia describes it, ACIM, or the *Course*, is a self-study that assists its readers in achieving spiritual transformation. It includes a text, which has 776 pages; a workbook section of 365 lessons; and a 75-page manual for teachers. Readers use the workbook each day for 365 days, or one year, to help them unlearn the way they see and think about everything. The Course intends to train the mind to change its perceptions and to decide to live life with love rather than fear. A *miracle* is a divine healing of human consciousness in which the ego's thinking is suspended and replaced with right thinking, or *right-mindedness*. Through forgiveness, the miracle occurs. Forgiveness is the central theme of the Course and has a broader meaning than you might think.

Helen Schucman and Bill Thetford wrote *A Course in Miracles* in 1965. Both Schucman and Thetford were professors of medical psychology at Columbia University. It seemed their weekly office meetings at Columbia Medical School had become argumentative and competitive. This negativity made them uncomfortable and upset. One afternoon, Thetford announced to Schucman, "There must be a better way." This declaration activated a series of dreams or visions in Helen, and in October 1965, a voice asked her to please take notes. This became *A Course in Miracles*. The many first-person notes taken by Helen and transcribed by Bill refer to the life and the teachings of Jesus and clearly identify him as the author. However, you do not need to believe this to benefit from the Course. It is not a religion but a universal spiritual teaching.

My studies over the past forty-odd years have given me many insights into the workings of this quandary we call *life*. I have never wanted to stop learning about the magnificence of the human *psyche* (meaning the "soul, mind or personality of a person," as Merriam-Webster describes it). I've read hundreds of books, gone to innumerable seminars and workshops, and traveled the world and discovered that all philosophical and metaphysical studies have very similar bases. I intend to simplify the many schools of thought and help bring you a pragmatic way to change your thinking and create paradigm shifts (*paradigm* meaning habitual patterns of focus) that allow more ease and joy into your life.

It's essential that you learn who you truly are if you intend to actualize a life of opportunity and possibility. The truth is that our intrinsic nature is perfect, unadulterated love. Love, as the Course interprets it, is total, always maximal, without degrees, distinctions, or selectivity. We are deservedly magnificent spirits in these human bodies. *A Course in Miracles* teaches that you never really die, and the truth (or right-mindedness) of our being is love and never changes. Everything other than that is an illusion. The Course also says the ego (or wrong-mindedness) is the sign of a limited and separated self, born in a body and doomed to suffer. The ego is insane and stands beyond the everywhere, apart from all. This dichotomy of the spirit and love on one hand and the ego and fear on the other hand is the story of good and evil. The power of creation has given us the free will of choice. In each and every moment, we can choose again. Fear or love is our only choice but permutable at any time.

As I stated earlier, we were born as perfect love and cannot change that truth. But we can remove what blocks our truth. One day at a time, one simple shift at a time, one loving thought at a time, we can live our truth. *A Course in Miracles* says that each of us chose the ego, this *tiny, mad idea*, of our fear-based mind, and this germ in our consciousness took over our physical existence. We then lapsed into fear, and it was like a decline from magnitude to littleness. The voice of this fear-based mind blocks our truth. Unlearning this false belief system, the negativity, the comparing, the lack, and the separation can reprogram our thoughts from ones of fear to ones of love. A *miracle*, as the glossary of *A Course in Miracles* written by Robert Perry states, is a divine healing of human perception, in which the normal "laws" of egoic thinking (based on guilt, fear, sickness, and death) are momentarily suspended.

"There is no order of difficulty in miracles." This is a direct quote from ACIM. The illusions of our fear-based minds tell us that one problem is harder to heal than others. The first principle of miracles states that the power of the Universe is always unlimited, sovereign, or absolute, as is the power of love. Contrary to our thinking, miracles are truly natural. When we can perceive our lives with love, we can create miraculous change.

Forgiveness

Through the experience of forgiveness, the miracle occurs. Through choosing the principles of forgiveness as our primary function, change takes place. This comes from the introduction to *A Course in Miracles*: "Nothing real can be threatened. Nothing unreal exists." Attack has no power to do real harm as the mind cannot attack, because what is real in you and in your attacker cannot be harmed or changed in any way. Emotional attack, then, has no effects. "It is a harmless mistake, a call for love/help." When someone appears to attack you, that attack seems to deprive you of something. You, in turn, seem to be the one in need, and rationalize attacking back to retrieve the dignity the assailant stole from you. But it's actually the other way around. The one in need is the attacker, for his attack actually pushes away the very love that the heart naturally desires. His assault leaves him feeling angry and in pain. At this turning point, he is to answer the call by giving love and understanding, as the Course teaches us. If he were true to his feelings, he would feel the need to correct his error or heal. When you realize that all of life is for healing, it makes the drama and hysteria you create at each uncomfortable turn completely unnecessary. What if you could see things differently and allow the possibility of forgiveness to be the vital perspective shift you need to create a life of fulfillment and joy? What if you could "turn the other cheek," as Christian doctrine describes? It's essential that you learn who you truly are if you intend to actualize a life of freedom and joy.

For-give-ness, as I like to understand it, is just this: *for-giving-love*, *for-giving-compassion*, *for-giving-understanding*, and so on. Simple as that may seem, it's always the answer. Forgiveness is really capable of amazing transformation in our lives, and freedom beyond our wildest dreams. It is not necessary to forgive the act necessarily. Mark Twain describes forgiveness as such, one of my favorite ways to decode this concept: "Forgiveness is the fragrance that the violet sheds on the heel that has crushed it."

We have been brought to this life to heal each other. Service is a top priority and is the real work we are all called to do. ACIM says that everything is for healing; even our lives themselves are for healing. With forgiveness in our hearts, we can truly experience the essence of who we are. It can release us from our fear and pain in order that we may experience oneness with each other and oneness with our spiritual essence. It can release us from our past and allow us to live more fully in the present. We can then live as the light that was intended and assist others by restoring our thinking and right-mindedness. This, as the Course states, leads directly and naturally to healing others. We must first be healed ourselves. Forgiveness is freedom.

The Course also chronicles that a *Holy Instant* is "when an ancient hatred becomes a holy Love and anger and resentment disappear." The hatred is no longer important or relevant, and you recalibrate to the energy of love or the Source. You can then breathe into the truth and begin to hear your inner voice, which will miraculously guide you in your day-to-day life. You absolutely cannot hear your inner guide when you consistently vibrate at a level of angst. Furthermore, the Course describes the ego as "suspicious at best, vicious at worst." We each have this threatening belief system within us. There is no better time in our planet's evolution than this to begin to understand how we were designed and improve our awareness of the spiritual laws so we create true success, while we reveal the Divinity within us.

Guilt—The Ego's Way

Guilt is the foundation of your consciousness here in this life, or so the ego would like you to believe. The ego uses this deceitful trick to keep you from your true nature or spiritual essence. The Spirit, being pure love, seems temporary and even too good to be true, especially when the bully in your mind relentlessly commands punishments for past mistakes. You have been taught over the years that guilt is a form of humility.

Conventionally, the word *humble* means having a low opinion of yourself, or unworthiness. The root of *humble* is *humus*, "ground or dirt," or the Latin *humilis*, "low or lowly." A true understanding of our infinite, boundless magnificence helps us see the arrogance, or false humility, of seeming to know more than the Divine, who created us for greatness. Do we really know better than our Creator? There are additional explanations of humility, such as *courteous, respectful*, and *not arrogant*.

The workbook lessons in ACIM compose a 365-day lesson plan to unlearn the blame and shame of past guilt and begin to understand the truth of consciousness. The lesson plan intends to guide and prepare you to see things differently and to respond to an error or mistake in a healthy way. This means exposing the underlying angst that keeps you from feeling *at-one-ment* with all the universality that surrounds you.

Guilt appears to have made our physical world, which is why the world also appears to be punishing us and the heart of our perception of it all. The Course states that guilt is the one and only cause of pain. The ego schemes to instill our continued separation and keeps us shackled to fear. The ego's attraction to guilt is founded in a real attack that causes spiritual guilt. Remember the Course's premise that minds cannot attack, for they are joined, and minds cannot be attacked, for they cannot be truly injured. The ego wants us to attack others to find safety or project our guilt onto another to relieve ourselves of its discomfort. Our many-sided perceptions create discomfort, and we abhor feeling uncomfortable. In reality, however, this only creates more guilt, which we all have an unconscious attraction to. If only we could let these assumptions go. The Course's teachings tell us that the journey to truth begins with learning and teaching the unreality of guilt through forgiveness.

The Special Relationship

Living in today's culture, we can easily believe that we will find happiness in external possessions, property, or wealth. Unfortunately, the more we accumulate, the more we want. This kind of living can make us feel faulty, as lasting happiness never accompanies all these material possessions. So, we turn to others to make us happy, hoping they will fill the void. The Course explains this as the "special relationship." The ego wants to be in control, so it keeps us looking outside ourselves for the love our souls so desperately need from our spirits. The ego knows it must provide some pretense of the love we really want, so it provides the special person with the special gifts. In fact, the Course shows us how we usually look to *shadow figures* (memories of people from our past who did not give us the special love we wanted from them) for these relationships. We attempt to replay our past, and if we don't get the specialness we want, we seek vengeance. What we are really doing is interacting with memories and mimicking painful beliefs from our histories. The ego continually sends us fear to keep us from our Divine Messenger, and it always communicates that we live in a cruel and unfair world. It wants us to constantly stay alert, or else we will be victims of these outside forces. The last thing the ego wants us to believe is that we can choose between fear and love, ego and spirit.

In the Course, *atonement* is referred to as recovering *at-one-ment*. It corrects perception and brings us back to our true essence, knowing that our separation was only an illusion. While the knowledge that the truth of our nature is one and the same as the Source or the Universe seems ungrounded, let's try to imagine the opportunity and freedom this supposition could instill in us.

ACIM aims to turn around the way we perceive or intuitively recognize the world. ACIM text uses unusual words or language, which, in the beginning, is very confusing. I studied it with a group and Robert Perry, the author and instructor who created the Circle of Atonement in Sedona, Arizona. Robert translated the text into seven volumes that make it easy to understand this profound chronicle.

Quite often, the text of Course in Miracles uses familiar words that seem to be used out of context., and the subject matter and lessons become very unclear and complicated. There is a very good reason for this. The meanings we ascribe to these words come from meaning we develop through what we see in our lives, in each other and the world. Our past experiences give rise to the meaning of words. It's necessary that we alter those very meanings, as they blind our sight and make us suffer. ACIM instills these terms with new, life-changing meanings and energetically recalibrates the old meanings' fearful (ego-based) implications. Over time and through repetition, we can learn to change the subconscious definitions we take for granted. The way we interpret our living world through language can confuse our communications if seen from the ego's illusions. Or we can illuminate it through the truth of the spirit to create real communication. That is distinctly what ACIM has done in the use of its terminology.

These principles that I have described are the most basic principles of *A Course in Miracles*. I hope I've made them fairly simple, my goal being to point out an alternative view to some of the ideology we believe and accept as truth. It's a very particular method of viewing the various aspects of our life challenges. These teachings and the possibility of another perception or alternative insight give us a fundamental understanding of how we were designed and why. If we are truly open to another way of viewing why so many of us suffer, then it's time to change our minds about what we see. "If nothing changes, nothing changes." ACIM is an ongoing inquiry and, as stated earlier, the remembering of our true nature of *Divine Love*. Deliberate focus and action are crucial to surrendering the guilt, through forgiving others, and leading us to universal love and peace.

Undoubtedly, *A Course in Miracles* has a lot more content to it. This book introduces you to the laws of nature and the metaphysical, spirited truths to initiate the necessary shifting and reworking of your ego-based, domineering mind. I want to expose you to a number of strategies, tools, and alternative practices so you perceive some paradigms that have become natural and habitual to you but do not serve you. It's paramount that you begin to create your life, rather than being a victim, and that you examine the possibilities of alternative patterns of perception. Your insights will expand exponentially as you expose yourself to this invaluable information. When all is said and done, as the proverb states, "Knowledge is power."

2

It's All about Energy

In the late 1980's, when I decided that I wanted to learn more about philosophy, I signed up for an at-home study with the University of Virginia. I received my syllabus with my course outline and many documents illustrating sound waves and an extensive study detailing energy and its principles. Confused but intrigued, I learned that there are three branches of philosophy, namely (1) natural philosophy, (2) moral philosophy, and (3) metaphysical philosophy. The abstruse metaphysical philosophy, which deals with the principles of being and knowing, interested me the most.

In the beginning, there was the Word, the vibration. Life and the experience of life were created through vibration or energy. Our thoughts produce feelings, which resonate with a specific vibration. Earth is a magnetic planet, and our emotional vibrations attract more of the same vibration.

The electrical current at the core of everything is creative energy or creative life force. The word *energy* comes from the Latin word *energeia*, from "en, in, within." Wikipedia describes this term, *energeia*, as potentiality and actuality. In philosophy, potentiality and actuality are principles of a dichotomy that Aristotle used to analyze motion, causality, ethics, and physiology in his physics. Okay, so rather than get too crazy with explanations and definitions, I would like you to understand the importance this internal energy has in your life. There are actually two types of energy, (1) materialized energy and (2) non-materialized energy. One can be seen, and the other is the invisible nature of something.

Deepak Chopra, the holistic physician, was the preceptor who truly made the nonmaterial field of *potentiality* a term of the times. I loved to hear him talk about potentiality, with his Indian accent, as if it was something you could have a conversation about over dinner. Well, actually, it is—*it* being the energy field that surrounds you and is within you and every living thing on this planet. We have many terms that describe this energy field—*Universe, life, Higher Power, Source energy, Divinity, Spirit, God,* and so on. Importantly, you need to understand the magnitude of the power we are discussing. This is the Source of life as you know it, and it has laws that you need to comprehend, appreciate, and be conscious of to create the life that you desire. That's right, create the life that you desire. This amazingly powerful energy that created you has given you the power to also create. We are all cocreators, but we just don't know it. Actually, we have created all along but have just not been aware of it. Just take note that *Infinite Intelligence* does not speak English, French, or any language; it only speaks energy.

I'm sure most of you have heard about or read *The Secret* by Rhonda Byrne. The book says the law of attraction is the Secret itself, and it brought a new awareness to many in our culture. "This simple and deliberate law states that every thought of ours is a real thing, a force". Like attracts like. We are physical beings who live on a magnetic planet. Because we also are human magnets, we attract according to our predominant thoughts, either loving or fear-based thoughts. The law of attraction is a very neutral law and doesn't discriminate. Whatever we see coming into our lives is attracted by the perceptions and images we hold in our minds.

Our most precious resource is therefore our attention and intention. It's a law that is absolute and constant. It has been said that whatever we think about most, we become. We'll delve deeper into these premises in the next few chapters.

The natural laws that dictate our lives unequivocally express a loving, benevolent energy that surges through our bodies and coordinates all the worldly creations that we see before us. We must master energy if we decide to be the deliberate creators we are meant to become. Otherwise, we will become victims of our default energy, and that can mean almost anything. Just like a computer, our operating system will assume a program when we, the user, don't specify an overriding action. Actually, most of the population is doing just that, as confusion and overwhelm run rampant. Just turn on the television or read a newspaper if you don't believe this. Victimization robs us of our natural inheritance of joy and freedom. If fear and doubt harness our thoughts, we create more of the same. It's therefore necessary that we become consciously aware of our power and the thoughts that we allow into our vibrational energy field. How do we do that? First, we must act deliberately and listen to our self-talk. This will assist us in discovering a new way to fundamentally change the criteria that have consistently created the existing templates we accept as normal or routine.

Development of Trust

Life, as I choose to call the omnipotent power within, loves you more than you love yourself. Frankly, this is one of the most valuable perceptions that you can envision your life through. You see, life has your back. Has anyone ever assured you of that or actually taught you the significance of this empowering statement? I'm always telling my friends and my coaching clients, "Life loves you and talks to you and guides you at all times, but you just don't pay attention."

We all experience life through the sentiment of our emotions, and to develop and cultivate trust in who we are and why we are here on this planet is, in actuality, our only mission and purpose in this life. Though it is mostly obscured from our emotional and intellectual understanding, our challenges play as important a role as our successes in deepening that trust, thus...It's All Good! Just knowing that everything is happening for your benefit and exactly the way it is designed to marks the beginning of this trustworthy process of evolving. Acknowledging the workings of our human psyche and physical body, gaining more knowledge in the spiritual laws, and realizing the energetic significance of vibrational magnetism can expand our confidence and expectations, bringing more miracles to our everyday reality.

The brain is physical, and the mind is nonphysical. Our physical experiences, through our senses, are brought to our brain by electrical sensors. Our five senses—(1) touch, (2) taste, (3) smell, (4) sight, and (5) hearing—convert into energy for the mind and brain. The mind cannot experience the physical world, so it uses the corporeal body to sense this dimension. Try to understand that the life we are attempting to experience is of the *Universal Creative Intelligence* and only one-dimensional realm. You see, the brain has done its job in this dimension but has reached its limit for other dimensions we may wish to explore. To experience something spiritual, we cannot use our physical brains and bodies. Through meditating, and allowing ourselves to integrate with the *universal Source energy*, we can attract energy for our dimensional bodies. More to follow.

Developing faith and confidence in a higher quality of life is possible, through not just thinking, not just understanding, not just believing, but *knowing* that self-mastery is attainable. Through desire, attention, intention, and trust in a power within, we can expect to find the all-encompassing sense of knowing. When we are in a state of knowing, we wholly align with our divine essence and can do just about anything.

I'd like to tell you a story about a profound revelation I had in 1993 when I was in Aguadilla, Puerto Rico, finishing up a master's course with a company I was working with, SAGE (Self-Actualization and Growth Exploration), owned by Walter and Peggy Dempsey. I was young and still a bit anxious about revealing my truths. Anyway, very early one morning, a bus took all twenty of us students to a desolate beach. We were asked to stay perfectly silent while there and to answer the question, "What does the Universe expect from you?" We were told to be ready to have a discussion when picked up later in the day. I'd be lying if I said I wasn't stymied. People were meditating and swimming, even diving off a dock. We played with feral dogs on the beach and studied them as they tried to rummage through the trash barrels. I believe it was three or four hours before they came back to pick us up.

It was very hot that day, and just as I saw the bus drive into the parking lot, I decided to take a quick dip. Defeated and discouraged, I ran into the water and just collapsed into the cool aqua. All of a sudden, I just knew—yes, I just knew the answer. The feeling of knowing was so big, so expansive, that it really didn't matter if I was right. As I floated in this majestic ocean at the tip of Puerto Rico, the buoyancy of the water supported me. The Universe expects to support us and asks nothing of us but to *feel good* and *let go*. I just let the sea carry me as the salt water was wafting me—a powerful experience I will always remember, as etched into my consciousness.

Along with acknowledging universal support, you must energetically align with this loving, magnanimous energy in order to receive the gifts that await your awakening. In the next chapter, I will detail the emotional scale to help you identify your feelings and the direction of your thoughts. In order to manifest the things your heart desires, you must energetically match to those desires' vibrations.

Enlightening your mind with loving thoughts and appreciation creates a steady flow downstream with the natural current of well-being. Allowing thoughts of fear and scarcity creates a flow opposite the natural flow and works against the current of life energy. That is why these feelings are so uncomfortable and laborious.

Most of us have adopted or inherited erroneous thoughts and patterns that actually create the majority of the vibrations that rule our lives. The subconscious mind is programmed with thoughts, feelings, and beliefs from conception to puberty. These thought patterns or paradigms are immature and fearful vows or beliefs that have deep roots in our past and hold us prisoner from the present, with very little hope for the future. Our core beliefs guide our lives and create the conversations in our minds that affect our thoughts. The statement "Our beliefs guide our lives" is the energetic engine that shapes the people, places, and things we see before us, as we attract what resonates with our inner thought and feeling energy. Uncovering our core limiting beliefs may seem daunting, but actually can be easy enough with a healthy desire and deliberate direction and practice.

I remember being at a seminar once that had this large banner on the wall that made a lasting impression on me. It said, "Yaguttawanna." Truer words were never spoken. We have to or gutta want to. I plan on guiding you to uncover those lies you tell yourself and open your mind to the bounty and inherent greatness that is your natural birthright.

Vibration: Resonating with Deep Emotional Memories and Feelings

If we are going to talk about energy and try to understand how it flows and creates, we now have to talk about vibration. Physics details a *vibration* as an oscillation of an electromagnetic wave.

I think it's also a good time to discuss thought and emotion. *Thought* is an idea or opinion produced by thinking. *Emotion* is described as an instinctive or intuitive feeling as distinguished from reasoning or knowledge. Neither emotion nor thought is specifically noted as a truth or a fact.

Another basic understanding of creation is that everything you see around the room you're sitting in began with a thought. Easy enough to accept, I believe. It may be a little harder to grasp that whatever you look at is actually a molecular structure of vibrational energy (an oscillation of an electromagnetic wave), just as you are. So, if you are going to master energy, you must absolutely understand how your thoughts resonate. It's therefore necessary to have conscious awareness of what you are thinking. To begin to sense our vibrational energy is key to designing a life that fulfills our heart's desire, our heart's desire being our soul's desire, as the heart and mind are allies.

Thoughts—Emotion—Actions—Momentum---Outcome

Our thoughts generate emotion, which gives rise to actions, which increases momentum to create an energetic vibrational outcome. This is the way the gravitational pull of our inner energy works. Each and every one of us was given this gift. But do we know that our unpredictable thought process must begin to become deliberate and intentional? Try to understand how we have allowed our false selves to keep us from the truth of who we genuinely are, spirits of pure love and potentiality, as we learned earlier. With the knowledge of this endowment, we can begin to make the necessary shifts to live as the light of life, vibrating with joy, empowerment, freedom, love, and appreciation.

It's also important to understand the energy that surrounds us, which can also influence our vibration. People, places, and things are susceptible to vibrational energy. We've just learned that we are energetic beings living in a magnetic world. Our actual energy field is called our *aura*. It radiates off the body anywhere from an inch to a couple of inches. When we walk into a room, our energy field affects every object in the room. All these material objects hold the energetic vibrations programmed by intellectual living beings. We can actually project our energetic frequency (happy, sad, mad, or glad) up to thirty-two feet. These objects do not have an intellect to help them decide what to absorb, so they take in whatever we give out. Like a sponge when it has fully absorbed all the energy possible, they start to radiate that energy out.

At one time or another, we've all walked into a room and felt comfortable or uncomfortable, not knowing why this was happening. Most of the time, we are unaware of what is happening. We actually receive an encoded message and decode it, but we aren't really aware of that. Even though we cannot see radio waves and wireless internet and cellular phone waves transmitting, we know they're there. Our brains decode these programmed objects with emotions, not words. Emotions are more of a universal language. All of life has these energies and programs. These energies are continually being configured, then destroyed over and over again. Everything—light, heat, music, and so on—is being absorbed, and energy is reassigned and created in something else.

Let me bring to light a new perspective accepted by leading-edge molecular biologists. Neuroscience has shown us that the conscious mind provides 5 percent or less of our conscious cognitive activity. It seems the unconscious mind is 95 percent responsible for our emotions, reactions, decisions, and conduct. At the cutting edge is Dr. Bruce Lipton, a former professor of medicine at Stanford University. Dr. Lipton states that the unconscious mind runs at forty million bits of data per second, whereas the conscious mind runs on only forty bits per second. He explains that the subconscious mind is an incomparable computer, programmed with a database of behavioral beliefs, most of which we learn before the age of six. It is now a proven fact that the unconscious mind rules our lives. Science recognizes that the mind and spirit play a primary role in who we are. "The subconscious mind cannot move outside its fixed program—it automatically reacts to situations with its previously stored behavior responses," says Dr. Lipton. Studies from as long ago as the 1970s explain that our brains begin to plan for a reaction just over a third of a second before we intentionally act. In plain English, even when we believe we are conscious, our subconscious mind is what actually regulates our perceptions.

The true power of consciously cocreating life is only found in the moment or, as Eckhart Tolle says, the now. You are a truly divine creature when in the now. The subconscious, core, limiting beliefs that you hold deeply buried, that keep you hostage, will not just disappear over time. Furthermore, the subconscious mind continuously overrides the conscious mind. Your unconscious past is an abyss that goes on forever. The present, or the power of now, is the only thing that can free you of the past.

Most of us are oblivious to the quite frightening truth that this age-old database runs our subconscious and shapes our lives. To begin to make changes, we must concern ourselves with the makeup of our unconscious thoughts, beliefs, and vows. Most unconscious programs that our minds continue to play are based in negativity and the fear of not being loved or worthy of what others think of us, and so on.

In order to be in the present moment, we must suspend or witness our subconscious mind. If we continue to allow our subconscious to dictate our thoughts and actions, it will anchor us to the past with almost no hope for the future, and no power in the present.

You have, at various times, unknowingly participated in the power of now, when, for example, you've been surrounded by a bucolic scene or listened to music you genuinely enjoy. While you're experiencing this, you actually drop your normal frame of reference for the present allowing a quiet mind and peacefulness to connect with universal consciousness. I'm pretty sure you can remember a time like this.

Dr. Lipton's studies show that we can change many things about ourselves and our core limiting beliefs by changing our interpretation of situations and events in our lives. Again, perception is multifaceted. Meditation, hypnotherapy, and other reprogramming advances have proven that we can actually change our brain's format or patterns by building new neural pathways with conscious thinking. We will address different examples of doing just that in the text that follows. What I'm attempting to do here by referencing this research is show you how these metaphysical premises are not ludicrous hypotheses but backed up by science itself.

3

The Emotional Scale and Its Guidance

My feelings are gauges of the power of my thoughts, which are the cause of my existence, or objective reality. There is nothing more consequential to me than how I feel. The following list comes courtesy of Abraham-Hicks.com.

1. Joy, empowerment, freedom, love, or appreciation
2. Passion
3. Enthusiasm, eagerness, or happiness
4. Positive expectation or belief
5. Optimism
6. Hopefulness
7. Contentment
8. Boredom
9. Pessimism
10. Frustration, irritation, or impatience
11. Overwhelm
12. Disappointment

13. Doubt
14. Worry
15. Blame
16. Discouragement
17. Anger
18. Revenge
19. Hatred or rage
20. Jealousy
21. Insecurity, guilt, or unworthiness
22. Fear, grief, depression, despair, or powerlessness

Our brain regulates the energetic being that we are and everything we see, feel, say, and do. It is the most sophisticated, intricate, extraordinary system ever known to humanity. Doesn't it make sense that, with this powerful creation we have been given, we should take some responsibility for learning how it works and how to use it to our advantage?

So, let's look at the metaphysical, psychological, and even physiological explanation for the brain and the mind. The brain, in simple terms, is the cerebrum or cerebral matter defined as the *intellect* or *intelligence*. The mind is the self-expression that contains the exceptional abilities of thought, awareness, and emotion and includes qualities connected to the heart.

As stated earlier, the mind is nonphysical; it should not be confused with the physical brain. *A Course in Miracles* assists us in understanding how the true mind is one with the spirit. It also helps explain how our minds can temporarily produce an untrue illusion or confusion, as in sleep or in misunderstood reactive behavior.

Most of us recognize the term *spiritual awakening* as commonly referring to a remembering of the mind before the ego was formed. Once awakened, the mind fully heals, and a shift in consciousness and a perception of a previously unconscious reality occur. The crowning moment of this revelation is the acknowledgment of oneness with all of life through awareness and that our true nature is whole, unbounded, and everlasting. The mind, brain, and body and the experience that comes with them in this world are the oscillations of consciousness. When we die, the oscillations disappear and rest in awareness with the capacity to evolve and recycle as experience. That leaves the soul body as pure consciousness. As Deepak Chopra has said, "The real you as pure consciousness is imperishable."

Universal Intelligence is the One Mind of all creation, the unconditioned Source of all life. All form arises from this One Mind or pure potentiality. This all points to an abstract energetic essence that shifts from possibility and timelessness to actualization, where experience occurs through the boundless diversity of form. Many metaphysical schools of thought say that we are all here on this planet for the "experience of life," to heal and to find the love in our hearts to share with and serve all humankind. That is our mission and purpose.

My personal life coach, Laura Fredrickson, simply and brilliantly would say that we live on a magnetic planet and, therefore, we are on a "vibrational Match.com" at all times. The realization that this profound statement is absolute and indiscriminate can legitimately change our reality. To manifest what we desire, we must vibrationally match and resonate the desired vibrations in the major part of our daily consciousness. We will learn that alignment with appreciation and gratitude is where our focus brings us to the highest vibration on this emotional register.

Focus—Deliberate Creation

Laura would also repeat time and time again, "Focus is our greatest commodity." What we focus our attention on expands—focus being what we are thinking and ruminating about over and over consciously and subconsciously. If you're wondering what your focus is, it's interpreted in what is presently before you, represented in your life. You just have to adjust your inner ratio of concentration so 51 percent focuses on what you prefer, and momentum will handle the arrangement.

As explained earlier, our thoughts create our feelings and become our natural GPS, the mental state that we assume and is vibrating and attracting the same vibration as the original feeling. Awareness of this fact always marks the beginning of change and freedom. But how can we change an outdated thought pattern if we're not aware of it?

Most of you are governed by what mainly comes from past reactions that have energetically designed your outdated operating system. Mistakes and wrong turns are generally caused by a subconscious *reaction* (the past) rather than a conscious awareness or *response* (the present). Reaction is always reacting to memories. Your subconscious mind is your reactive mind; your conscious mind is your responsive mind.

Knowing that how you feel is what mostly inspires your experiences, wouldn't it be beneficial to be more deliberately conscious of which guidance system directs your energy? After all, becoming a deliberate creator is your human birthright, and the most important thing you can do is "feel good" if you want to vibrate with the feel-good emotions that will continue to attract more and more feel-good emotions and situations.

Understanding that your focus can transform your energy, isn't it smarter to focus on what you want, rather than what you don't want? Whenever I ask my clients what they really want, they almost always start with what they don't want. Surprise, surprise when what you don't want shows up. Universal Law, at your service …

The top seven emotional scale indicators gauge feelings of alignment with the flow of life. Many metaphysicians use the metaphor of flowing down a stream or river to explain the natural flow of life energy. When you are in the flow, you feel the natural current of alignment with the Universe. When you feel appreciation for the better part of your day, you know you are in alignment. Some athletes call this *the zone*, or artists call this *the pocket*. The lower indicators on the scale represent a lack of flow or the tension of pushing against the current. We all know where that takes us. That's right—nowhere!

The emotional scale gives us a template for monitoring our emotional vibrations. If we are going to succeed at keeping our vibration aligned with the higher energetic feelings on the scale, we need to gauge our vibration at various times during the day by recognizing or checking in with how we feel. Practicing this helps us become more aware of the energetic pull of our thought process. When we start focusing on some of these higher vibrations, we should see results very quickly. The more we can laser focus, the quicker we can manifest results. Being more intentional with our thoughts and feelings creates greater well-being.

When you start to become more vigilant or watchful of your thoughts, you will see that most are just repetitive or habitual. Make a point of becoming aware of them. All you have to do to become aware is to *decide* to be aware. A decision has movement or momentum. Begin to become a more deliberate designer in your life.

"What You Resist Persists"

When I learned this powerful phrase, I really began to see miracles appear. It's not easy to decipher, but it is very simple. When a negative thought pops up, immediately stop it, and move on to a more positive one. Don't even entertain the thought. I remember when I quit smoking, I found success only by not entertaining the thought of a cigarette for even a second.

Numerous negative influences surround you in your everyday life—news on the TV, friends, your imagination, and so on. Whenever you become aware of these negative influences, say, "Stop!" Just turn them down instantly. There shouldn't be any resistance involved. If you do find a strong resistance to this particular negativity, then face that resistance head-on, with no resistance. Examine it with detachment, and bring it to light; ask the right questions. Ask yourself, "Why is this here, and what is this really?" and understand what powers it. Doing this necessary undertaking, you can overcome it. Healing being a big part of existence, you can let go of an old, limiting illusion and make room for something good to fill that energetic pocket in your psyche. Remember, there is really nothing but love; everything else is imagined.

4

Shifting Our Paradigms

Tony Robbins says that power "is the ability to act." Taking deliberate action changes the way you experience the world. However, sometimes, you become stuck in old default imprints in the mind–brain paradigm. You can become a biological robot as your mind wants to live with the familiar and run the show from the only point of view you believe possible. Do you really want to be a victim of autopilot energy? Wouldn't you rather become a deliberate creator? All it takes is a simple conscious change of thought, which creates a new feeling, which alters your vibration, which can attract more of what you desire.

You are in charge of your thinking and your brain, not the other way around, and the mind–body connection always has a physical component. All responses and reactions start in the brain. Your old beliefs, wounds, and habitual behaviors are controlled there, instead of the other way around. The mind is like the hard drive; the body is the software. When the mind is stuck in old tendencies, the software cannot change. Again, awareness is the solution. If you're aware, you can take back control.

Deliberate, concentrated awareness of our emotional vibration can metamorphose our unconscious perceptions. This awakening is very similar to a profound change, like a caterpillar becoming a pupa, which then becomes an adult butterfly. With deliberate, concentrated effort and focus, we can rightfully soar above our perceived flaws and errors.

Witnessing and Integrating

Seeing yourself with clarity and without clutter in every situation has been called *witnessing*. This particular form of consciousness happens in the moment, in the here and now, and apart from the subconscious. Power is only in the now, remember! The majority of your thoughts fundamentally follow your tribally or culturally programmed subconscious ideology. To begin to get clear and gain back your brainpower, you can witness, or stand apart from, the inner chatter and observe your robotic reactions and the plethora of thoughts that are constantly running, like a ticker tape rolling through your mind. Believe it or not, you can actually pick and choose which thoughts you'd prefer.

With this practice, you can change the old and bring in the new awareness of your inner consciousness and true essence. You can literally change your mind, change your energy (vibration), and change your outcome.

Ordinarily, people believe that they are their thoughts and beliefs. You're not your mind. The mind is a powerful tool to be used, not identified with. Use it to think right, and shut it down when you're not using it.

The truth of our authentic nature is hidden under our subconscious mind's immature (egocentric) belief system. When we witness these programmed reactions, pause, and see them for what they truly are— conjecture, speculation, and learned behaviors—we can choose to *integrate* the disowned parts of ourselves and respond with true, loving thoughts. It's usually our wounded inner child, deep within our heart, that is looking for the attention that we have avoided for a very long time. We mustn't disown our false self or judge it, as the Spirit accepts all our errors. As ACIM simply states, all sin is a mistake and an error in judgment.

In 1988, John Bradshaw, the educator and author, wrote *Healing the Shame That Binds You* and hosted a PBS television series that referenced addiction, recovery, codependency, and spirituality. He became extremely relevant and gained quite a bit of notoriety. The gist of his study involved the analysis of toxic shame and the inner child.

We are born into this world in perfect innocence. Over a short period of time, we develop this shame-based self, or the "soul murderer," due to parental and outside influences. Please understand Bradshaw does not condemn our caretakers, as most of them were victims themselves.

It is extremely important to acknowledge these lost pieces of your inner child that you ignored. Bradshaw teaches that you can heal those parts of yourself that you have abandoned and shamed through the mirrors of your teachers, your parents, and more. His main premise is to embrace the inner child and the wounded parts of yourself that you have so harshly neglected throughout your life. (See it as a call for love, as ACIM describes it.)

Healing the Shame That Binds You would have us picture ourselves sitting at a large conference table with the angry and abandoned fragments of our confused inner children. While there, Bradshaw would have us speak tenderly to all the inner children. At first, the children will not really trust us, but over time, that will change.

As we build a loving relationship, it's important that we be genuine adults who set boundaries for our inner children, these pained pieces of ourselves who are basically immature and want instant gratification. These wounded parts of us go unconscious or abuse themselves with unhealthy behaviors like drinking, eating, and so on. These are the children we lock away in dark places inside us, and these are the wounds that control our lives. These inner children are really our broken-down soul and the entryway to our spiritual self.

The integration process includes a consciously developed loving relationship with all our inner children, so we begin to validate their feelings and let them know that things will be different. By owning and honoring all parts of ourselves, we can now begin to have some balance and harmony within, healing our broken hearts, which have been dictating our reactive lives.

In truth, we have deceived, forsaken, and depraved ourselves. This is out-pictured in irrational reactions to situations we are involved in or people we are dealing with at any given moment. If we can withhold judgment at these inopportune times and witness the situations without attachment, we can realistically be brought to peace and sever the hold of our false selves. It is our belief system that keeps us troubled and our soul's spirit that brings us peace. This is how our emotional defense system works. I will go into more detail in the next section.

Perception and Projection

As we understand it, *perception* is the ability to understand something through our five senses. It can also be an insight through intuition or memory.

It appears that events and things outside ourselves produce our perception of them, although our own belief system, especially our self-image, actually creates our perceptions (projection makes perception). How we identify with the world is what establishes the circumstances we experience.

Trust that life has your back and continually demonstrates where you need to heal through people, places, and things that present themselves to you, as they become a mirror for life's lessons. Through your experiences and your conscious awareness, you can witness what appears to be outside you and out of your control. You commonly believe that your perceptions are caused from without and that external things give information to your brain through your senses. In actuality, your limited belief system, mostly shaped by your ego, influences them.

As Bradshaw taught, integration is vitally necessary. In truth, your core beliefs that guide and attract you to see things internally cause your perceptions. Think about how many times you have told yourself something disheartening, and *boom*, proof has come before your very eyes.

Projection is the ego's way of keeping us in fear and separateness. Remember separateness is the ego's main job through guilt and angst. As physical beings, we abhor being uncomfortable and therefore use projection to relieve ourselves of those annoying, judgmental, disowned beliefs and feelings. Once we expel them, usually in an irate rant, we feel guilty, which creates more discomfort, and the misery and confusion continue.

Let me explain how the ego uses projection to keep you separate. Say you throw out an idea through your internal mind, into the presumed external world. It appears to be outside you. For example, you tell your friend that she has been selfish. She and her selfishness appear to have given you the pain you seem to feel. But in actuality, you have attracted what your *perception* tells you is a selfish friend. If you wanted to do the work to learn a lesson, and believed you attracted this selfishness, you would question where within yourself you've attracted or projected this feeling. If you can ask the question, you will usually find the answer. After all, our vibration attracts more of the same, and this perception of a selfish person wouldn't be in your face, so to speak, if you weren't energetically attracting it.

This is an opportunity not to judge yourself or the other person, but to gauge your vibrational activity, to become aware of the direction of alignment within your resonance.

Remember earlier you learned that life is for healing and life loves you unconditionally, so let's also remember that forgiveness is always the answer. Forgive yourself for the error in perception, and forgive your friend for falling prey to your energy or projection. "A bitter pill to swallow," says the ego, but I like to say it's just a call for love.

One of the most profound turnarounds in my spiritual quest came when I learned, "Your perception of me is a reflection of you; my reaction to you is an awareness of me." Life, Divinity, and the Universe love us and are constantly giving us opportunities to heal and grow. Through the law of attraction, our vibration has shown us the place in our heart and soul that needs forgiveness, integration, and healing. I know it's a lot to absorb, but keep reading, and please keep an open mind.

Guilt is the ego's middle name, and fear is its last name. Try to remember that when those feelings arise, the illusion is the ego's web. The only real truth is the Spirit's infinite love.

We accept most of our assumptions as truths, when, in reality, they are just perceptions of truths. So no time like the present to actually look at what is true. ACIM describes *truth* as what is true, real, factual. It's indivisible, changeless, and constant. It cannot be destroyed, perceived, or believed; it can only be known. "Truth is only joy and safety." The Course also states, "The truth about us is grandeur and perfection." The opposite of truth is illusion, or a false perception of reality.

As part of the path in our existence here on this earth, we must search out resistance to the laws that govern our physical and spiritual world. Our sojourn here is to discover the truths over illusions and bring darkness to light. The reality that "what we resist persists" can help us relinquish our attachment to our buried pain. In actuality, we don't get what we want in life; we get what we believe. What we think of and see as lacking in our life is usually what we resist within our belief system.

Beliefs

I learned at the very beginning of my metaphysical studies that "beliefs guide your life," and I've never forgotten this enlightening statement. Your outdated, limiting beliefs in your spiritual evolution may be driving you to places you really don't want to go. They have become part of your default imprint in your mind and brain.

So, you ask, how do you decipher your beliefs? You listen to what you say, as words are powerful, and you stop and listen to the self-talk in your mind. Are you someone who tells yourself, "That's not for me," "I'm not smart enough," "I don't deserve it," and so on? I would guess that most of the time, you're not even aware of your self-talk. It can become quite a skill, over time to tune in and become aware of what you tell yourself. Shifting gears from negative to positive does get easier with desire and patience. Remember it's a practice and begin to acknowledge the process of improving your self-love.

To begin to build awareness of what you say to yourself and others throughout the day is an invaluable tool. Strive to listen to the words that come out of your mouth, and rather than just speak to speak, be more vigilant about your speaking and storytelling. Words and your speech have immense power. Listening to both your self-talk and your language will even help you develop the skill of listening, a talent necessary to practice many life skills, as you become more aware and tune in to your inner guide. But do remember that words do not teach; it is experience that teaches.

Beliefs are very similar to convictions or opinions that you've adopted from past experiences. They are really just thoughts that you think over and over. My Apple computer's dictionary states an *opinion* is "a belief or judgement that rests on grounds insufficient to produce complete certainty." So, in actuality, these beliefs that guide your life can be uncertain or untrue even though you've adopted them and allowed them to dictate your experiences. Most of your beliefs are not the truth; they are simply your perception of the truth. Beliefs are not good or bad. You just want to understand the ones that serve you and the ones that do not.

Our self-talk can at times be brutally cruel and unloving. I know I've discovered some shaming phrases that I unconsciously tell or told myself—"You're not worth it," "You'll never have it," "There's not enough," ad infinitum. You can change these self-defeating allegories, buried deep inside your heart, that you tell yourself. You can reveal these untruths you've adopted as "your stories" that manifest as your limiting beliefs and work with your ego to keep you beaten and separate. It's time to tell another story and know that you can! One of my favorite children's stories is *The Little Engine That Could*. I read this to my children and hoped it would instill in them a *knowing* of the power of belief and perseverance. If you believe you can and feel the joy of accomplishment in your bones and your sinews, the Universe responds through cause and effect. Becoming aware of and specifying your desires can result in situations that make you feel good and we know at this point that feeling good is a major catalyst for more feeling good and more feeling good. It's the beginning of shifting your outlook and outcome. I'd like to quote Yoda, from *The Empire Strikes Back*: "Do. Or do not. There is no try."

So much of life has affected your beliefs—parents, teachers, kids, television, and so on. They can be like blindfolds to you. I am asking you to become aware of this paradigm and consciously choose what to believe, whether it involves your abilities, your health, your finances or your relationships. Let go of the self-defeating outdated emotional downloads. Making the choice to place your attention on what you actually prefer to think and conceive, will facilitate a more aligned, more loving and a more purposeful belief system, that will manifest more of the same. After all, like attracts like. What an endowment to finally realize that if you really want to change anything in your life, *you* have to change, and change from the inside out.

Vision

Another means of deciphering your unconscious proclivity is to take stock of your life's vision and what you see before you, as the law of attraction consistently brings your thoughts and beliefs to you. I titled my coaching enterprise REALeyes NOW, my tagline being "REALeyes your best life," as I intend to guide you to see life through your REALeyes, or your divine Spirit's eyes, rather than your egocentric (vain, narcissistic, and judgmental) eyes. "When you change the way you look at things, the things you look at change." I just love this simple truth.

You wonder why your energy is low or down. You wonder why things aren't always as they seem or the way that you would like them. Knowing these adjustments in the way you think and feel can change your energetic vibrations. It can begin to help you more easily make the changes necessary to become the co-creator you were meant to be. Knowing who you truly are, and especially your potential to build a life of freedom and joy, becomes more realistic than wishful thinking.

The time is now to get beyond the pain and pleasure or the psychological archetype that has been our frame of reference for understanding behavioral modification. Science can absolutely be adjusted to include the incredible power of what lies within. Rather than looking outside ourselves for change to take place, we can open the door to our true substance, our souls and spirits, and the voice of the guide within.

See the majesty and love that surround you, even when they may not appear to be there. It doesn't matter what is out-pictured in your life, because it all reflects your state of consciousness, and consciousness can change and adjust. Deliberately choose to have fun with life. Life is joy! The essence of life is joy. The gift of creation is abundant where there is joy.

Look around you; nothing can exist before it first exists and you see and feel it with your mind's eye. You get where you want to go in your mind first. It's simple. Anything you wish to see or have, have it in your mind first.

Affirmations

The very first thing I coach my clients to do is to understand that words have enormous power. Even the Bible states, "In the beginning there was the Word," the vibration of a teeny-tiny particle that created more of itself with intent. "The Word was with God and the Word was God."

Creation and its workings happen like this: *being* determines *thinking*, which determines *speaking*, which determines *action* or *doing*, which also causes the system to receive and experience what was created in our being and thinking. Being, so you see, is the first cause of any state. In actuality, we can only *be* in a state; we cannot *do* a state or *speak* a state. Being is consciousness, and being is of no mind. Sometimes, the mind can destroy what we are being. The best way to be during the day is to be of no mind. Be an observer, not a thinker. Don't identify with the mind; identify with the universal *being*.

Most people don't tend to the first three steps of being, thinking, and speaking. They just work and work and work and then wonder why they aren't successful. The final step of creation is *action*. Actions are part of the Word, but the role they play is to receive what we have already created on the other three levels. Actions don't create the experience; the mind creates the experience. Most don't even think to use the Word. The Word invokes the laws of the Universe. They are not just spiritual laws; we can prove them scientifically using quantum physics.

Masaru Emoto, a Japanese doctor of alternative medicine, was the first to explain and illustrate how words could change the molecular structure of water. He exposed droplets of water to various words, music, and environmental changes, then froze the water and examined the frozen crystals under a microscope. Positive words and emotions and classical music created beautiful crystals while negative words and emotions and heavy metal music created misshapen crystals.

Once we have determined what energetic vibration our subconscious is creating, we can decide if that energy is what we would choose. If it isn't, we can reprogram the subconscious, with thoughts that express a higher vibration with an improved result. Of course, you need to believe that what you want is possible in order to actually make that new belief resonate. Another tool you can use to do that is an affirmation. An *affirmation* is a declaration of something positive or true. Repeating more positive, loving, affirmative statements over time creates a resonance that can feel so much better than your habitual mind chatter and can quickly become an integral part of your life force. Most of the time, we repeat negative statements in our minds— "I hate my job," or "I just can't do that"—which creates or attracts through vibration more of what we don't want. Positive statements, consciously designed—such as "I am free," "I am safe," and "I am loved and loving"—can bring us more of what we do want. They can shape our limiting beliefs and create the positive affirmations, or truths, that can now actually become an integral part of us.

Words have power, and life-affirming words create positive feelings that create positive vibrations, drawing to you more beneficial situations and conditions, and who doesn't want more of those?

I suggest you deliberately create your own affirmations that mean something to you and are emotionally driven, as they can put you in the flow with very little effort. It doesn't really matter if the affirmations are not true yet. You can repeat them over and over until you've embedded them in your subconscious mind, and they become your reality.

The Art of Allowing

A powerful affirmation to start with is "I am willing to change." Willingness is the beginning of allowing. The art of allowing pretty much means just accepting things as they are. When we allow people, places, and things to be as they are, without judging them or trying to fix or change things, we are able to tap into the art of allowing. Most of us have never learned how to allow. We've been trained to take action, work harder, run faster, fight harder, or change things if we don't like them.

Here I am, telling you to allow life to flow with its brilliant natural intentions, and the trick is to play with this omnipotent potentiality and get better and better at trusting it and feeling better and better about that trust. By doing this and consciously choosing concepts that feel good, you can actualize vibrational alignment with the Source energy. When you are in a state of truly allowing, you consistently feel good, thereby attracting and manifesting more things to feel good about. This concept of letting go or *allowing* is what opens the portals so that the Source of well-being can flow to you and through you, and should not be overlooked. Your inner being is consciously accessible if you allow it.

Remember to always speak in the present tense: "I am," "I have," and so on. *I am* is a declaration of being in the here now. Our subconscious mind is our trusted messenger who will always bring us what we ask for. If we speak in a future tense— "I want," "I hope for"—we get just that, want and hope, period. We must be willing to change our verbiage, change our thinking, and change the stories we tell about ourselves, about who we are. To be willing to do this alone opens portals for all sorts of possibilities. Healthy, positive affirmations are extremely helpful in recalibrating and shifting our old restrictive patterns. Deliberately thinking of and repeating life-affirming statements conditions our conscious minds and creates new channels in our subconscious minds, giving vision to a more desirable life. In the next chapter, we will delve deeper into our conceptual thinking methods.

The Universe loves clarity, so dig deep, be honest, and recognize the feeling; then refer to the scale. Identifying with one of the first seven selections is much more beneficial than identifying with the others below. Notice that gratitude and appreciation are the highest vibrations. A quick and easy way to get yourself to vibrate at higher frequencies is to wake up every day and make a list of what you are grateful for. This will bring more and more to you to appreciate, which, in turn, will bring you more joy, freedom, love, and empowerment. Your goal through these studies is empowerment. This takes you out of the victim role and allows you to take more responsibility for creating your own life. The scale can be an invaluable tool, if combined with intention and commitment, so as to make it a conscious, consistent part of your life.

To make it simple, you can check in emotionally, being very clear, using the scale. Once you identify your vibrational mind-set, with honesty and clarity, you can begin to adjust or enhance and compose more life-giving, affirming thoughts and feelings. You can also receive other bonuses from having awareness of who or what is running the show at various times during the day, as this inquiry can unveil your limiting unconscious beliefs and archetypes. With this knowledge, and these few techniques, you can unquestionably begin to transition your patterns in a more authentic nature.

Contrast and Its Purpose

Why can't we just have everything we want? Well, if we didn't live a life of contrast, we wouldn't actually know what we really want. *Contrast* is variety, diversity, and so on, the wanted and unwanted. Variety assists us in making a conscious choice; it gives us the opportunity to express our unique selves. Contrast is essential to our growth and expansion; it gives us a chance to fully attend to and evaluate something, and then decide what we, in truth, really want. And it creates vibrational, emotional energy for the process of attaining that desired result.

Problematically, as they wait for their desire to manifest, most people look at *what is*. What is being interpreted by a misguided energy may not be what we really desire. This supposed roadblock creates doubt and resistance and pushes away our desired result. The secret to this dilemma is to think about our desire fulfilled. We can create momentum if we repeatedly and consistently focus on the having what we desire and, more importantly, *why* we want it. The why is the impetus and inspiration for the desired result. Do not think about how or when or where; that just creates resistance and struggle—*resistance* being a belief that we will get what we want by pushing against this condition or that situation—and this disallows the Universe's natural flow.

As we have learned, it's all about energy and mood, attitudinal work, and how we feel. I can't stress this enough. Contrast is necessary for focus. Enjoy the variety, as we can't explore good if we don't know bad, can't know clarity if we haven't experienced confusion, can't know distance if we haven't experienced closeness. Embrace it because sameness is boring. You must understand that as we are creating the problem, we are creating the answer too.

After all, we would have no expansion or development in our lives if we only experienced what we want. Our lives are about the thrill of the physical experience and repeatedly coming into alignment with expansion, alignment and expansion, alignment and expansion. We came here for the joy of the ride, not to get things done, and joy's triumph of that ride is fashioned out of contrast.

Everything is already created, and the Source always knows what we want and holds it for us, while or until we align our vibration with the vibration of the desire. Life then becomes more of an adventure than a challenge. Our way of life becomes richer and sweeter and more delightful. Enjoy the emotional swing, because knowing what we do not want brings us closer and closer to what we want.

5

Consciousness

Consciousness, simply defined, is the ability to be awake and aware of one's surroundings. It is the mind's awareness of itself and the world (as defined in a dictionary description I found on Google). It is not an easily defined term, as many brilliant psychologists have agreed. But rather than spend time with this confusing conundrum, we will accept the simple definition for our study here.

A human being has only one brain and one mind. That one mind has two very different operating systems. People have given many labels to the mind's two distinct powers—for example, the voluntary and the involuntary, the conscious and the subconscious, the objective and the subjective. For our purpose, we will use the terms *conscious* and *subconscious*.

The Conscious Mind

Wikipedia defines the *conscious mind* as "the state or quality of awareness, the ability to experience or feel, wakefulness, having a sense of selfhood or soul." Consciousness is the primary substance of all things. A change of consciousness can change your life, as it is the only substance of life. If, for example, you perceive problems in your life, they are a manifestation of consciousness. Of course, the opposite is also true. Peace and joy are embodied by the conscious awareness of the authentic truths of humankind.

The light of life is consciousness. The biblical quote "All things are made manifest by the light and everything made manifest is the light" is the one and only reality.

The great prophet, author, and teacher Neville Goddard studied the biblical scriptures and taught the truths of these philosophical teachings. He interpreted and clarified their abstract significance. He brought to light the concept that the center of consciousness is the feeling of I Am. "I Am" is God's self-definition. I remember from religious schooling that when Moses saw the burning bush on the Mount, as the Bible describes, he approached it, and it spoke to him, first asking him to take off his sandals, as this was a holy place. Moses asked, "Who are you?" and the burning bush replied, "I Am, that I Am."

You don't have to advocate for religion to study ancient scripture and its philosophical meaning. An uncomplicated way to describe the Bible is as a clear and understandable example of divine inspiration, a document that describes the relationship between the universal life force (God) and humanity.

The idea of "I Am" as the Source of consciousness assists us in understanding our sacred essence. This holy attribute resides in the center of all beings. It is the absolute birthplace of our consciousness. Good or bad, we all create our lives through consciousness. The arrangement of the mind—rich or poor, happy or sad—and the different arrangements of particles, protons, and electrons create our consciousness. Only by a change of consciousness can we change our self-concept.

A Course in Miracles teaches us that consciousness is the ego's target. Consciousness can receive communications from the ego, hidden in the subconscious, or from Divinity, which is also hidden from the conscious mind. We must then choose between the two voices. Our consciousness can be taught to experience miracles and recognize the unlimited world of potentiality and possibility through Divinity, or to recognize the limited world of lack or scarcity through the ego. This deliberation can make the difference between being the essence of the real world of happiness and joy and being the essence of the illusionary world of fear and guilt. The conscious and subconscious minds are just two impartial domains of activity within one mind, influenced by the ego or Divinity. The villain sits on one shoulder and the angel on the other.

The Subconscious Mind

In simple terms, the *subconscious mind* is the mind of God or Christ's consciousness. It is our unbounded holistic mind. The subconscious mind is also the accumulation of assumptions and suppressed, repressed, unconscious, hidden memories of the past. This is where our inner child hides away.

I'm sure you hear a bit of contradiction in that explanation. The exciting part of this commentary is that it is a dual-edged force that commands and reacts. More importantly, though, this enormously powerful subconscious mind can be trained. It's crucial that we become aware of which part of the mind influences our thoughts and feelings at any given time.

It's really very simple, but it's not very easy because memories of past experiences trigger habitual behaviors, and once again, we find ourselves in struggle and suffering, that old familiar paradigm. *A Course in Miracles* lesson 2 confirms, "I have given everything I see all the meaning that it has for me". Do you really want to live from the limiting beliefs of the past (fear), or do you choose to come from a place of possibility and the now (love)? If you become unbalanced, just ask yourself, "Am I coming from a point of love or of fear?" This can be a crucial tool in your enlightenment. Remember also that in each and every moment, you can choose again. This uncomplicated acknowledgment can truly change your reactive behaviors so you welcome a healthy peace of mind that is your natural birthright.

The Law of Assumption

Goddard began his teaching by introducing the law of assumption, the truth being that what you see in this energetic, material world is not necessarily what you truly see but what you *assume* to see. You may find this baffling, but you live in an assumptive world. As time went on, this prophet of a man truly lived *The Law* and then realized *The Promise*: "Imagining creates reality." These two metaphysical principles, *The Law* and *The Promise*, were written in text as far back as 1961. They completely changed my perspective in the thick of many mind-altering premises in the study of spirituality.

The Gift of Imagination

Goddard taught that no external change can take place until you first have an imaginal change. So essentially, if you presume that a man can call forth that which he can vividly imagine of whatever he chooses, with a perception of what he sees as real as nature, then he is the master of his fate. Goddard educated his followers to believe that to do this, you must mentally abandon yourself to the wish fulfilled in your love for that state, thereby living in a new state. The secret is self-abandonment, a letting go of your fear based self. You must embody and *love* a new state of awareness. You must live in that state because you cannot truly commit to what you do not love. Committing to the feeling of the wish fulfilled and thinking from it, with conviction and love, must have an inevitable result because imagining creates reality.

Imagination is both conservative and transformative. It's conservative when it builds its world from memories of past perceptions and the five senses. It's transformative when it creates the imagined desired intention from a present sense and the person thinks *in* it and thinks *from* it. If thinking from a remembered image, one is thinking *out of* it and thinking *of* it. The point is, if you enter *into* the imagined, you can know that which is creatively transformative, realize the desired intention and feel the joy it brings physically and mentally, and therefore give birth to the desired aspiration.

This, of course, is a challenging but not an unimaginable realization. It may seem arduous because we normally spend very little time, in our adult lives, in our imagination. Neville Goddard's principles present a bounty of seeming miracles. He helps us enhance our understanding of consciousness while introducing us to a new relationship to Divinity that we can find just beyond our physical sight.

Imagination is spiritual consciousness. Sacred imagining and human imagining are in themselves only one power, and the ultimately essentially nonobjective reality. "Objective reality" writes Johann Gottlieb Fichte, the renowned German philosopher, "Is solely produced through meditation." and so it seems evident that humankind is imaginably creating the situations of life either knowingly or unknowingly. We pay way too little attention to our invaluable gifts, and the time is *now* for us to begin to remove the obstructions and the resistance to the miraculous gifts of consciousness that were bestowed on humankind. Imagination might very well be the greatest gift of all and the heart of creation.

In Goddard's commentary *The Law*, he talks about a child's make-believe and remaking the world according to your heart of love and trust. He says, "Nothing stands between you and the fulfillment of your dreams but facts, and facts are the creations through imagining." He enlightens you to uncover the essence of reality, while you must affirm either the "way of the imagination or the way of the senses." There is no space for impartiality.

Humankind and the past are one, with facts that hide deeply below the conscious mind. To humankind, these seem forgotten, but they are *not*; they're memorized and persistent, and they still exist. Our job is to revise and reverse the error or mistaken perception of the ego-driven, fear-based memory. We must go back to the disavowed remembrances and nullify the ego's vicious, malicious renderings; the false, fearful self (keeping us down and separate); and the lie we live. Goddard calls this process a *revision*, which produces a *repeal*. I like to think of it as an act of forgiveness, performed with the Spirit's support, creating a Holy Instant and a return to love. To truly change our lives, we must change our past. Knowing that our present images create our consistent nuisances, we can reimagine the past, or revise the vision of scenes where we forgot who we essentially were and are, awakening to the illusion of ego-based fear and separation and accepting the truth of only love. In truth, love has no opposite, ACIM says, and explains that we cannot learn it, only welcome it, through earthly love or forgiveness.

6

The Time Is Now

The truth of the matter of time is that the only time that really exists is now. Believe it or not, the past, the present, and the future are only an illusion. The best part of this conundrum is that, once you understand that you create this illusion, you can consciously and deliberately change how you perceive it. Time flows in all directions; the past, present, and future are all happening at the same time. Einstein's theory of relativity states that we can slow down time or even go back in time, but we are not going to study the science of time. We're just going to explore time with open minds and expanded consciousness and begin to become more aware of the illusion of time.

This moment, the one that you are mindful of right now, is the eternal moment of now. We can remember the past and dream about the future, but we can only *exist* now. As we touched on earlier, the present moment is one of the greatest gifts we have. It is where all the energetic power lies. It allows us to change our past thoughts, words, and actions. There, we can experience the self, and if we are consciously aware and trusting enough, we can see, with our REALeyes, the healing or the lessons that we truly need in order to clean up our vibrational alignment with life-affirming, better-feeling energy.

Let's decide right now to be mindful, cognizant, and enlightened in the moment, with no memory of the past that blinds us to what truly is or can be. Let's practice detachment but feel secure and self-assured in our choices and intentions, and a brilliant world will open up before our eyes.

ACIM's very first of the 365 lessons are designed to help us unlearn that everything we see in our material world is riddled with memories of every time we saw or sensed that object or had a similar experience in our past. These impressions taint our perceptions, and the simple act of awareness can give us an opportunity to make a better choice in every moment.

Imagination is great for creating our future, but only by living in the present can we get to our desired tomorrow. Let's remember that the Universe can only use the present moment to send us opportunities, people, and evidence of our vibrational attraction. With conscious awareness, we can choose a *better feeling*, if need be, and advance. If we consistently see the truth in the now with clarity and love and take responsibility for everything we have already created in our world, without blame or judgment, we can see our lives as symbols of the inner self and use this to strengthen our consciousness.

As the Buddha says, "Concentrate the mind on the present moment."

Time is only a concept of the mind. If there is no mind, there is no time, so let's enter the realm of timelessness by eliminating constant control of the mind. Let's look into more mindful meditation even in our wakeful lives. Play with the thought of just *being*. More and more people are doing that practice and becoming more aware of its importance.

We all can choose to live passively, due to old paradigms or habits that imprison us. Or we can wake up and participate fully, even if we don't always like what is happening at any given moment. Our essence is love and we are loved more than most can imagine, and we are continually guided to use our gifts and powers, if we just take the time to be aware and use the endless, boundless energy at our fingertips.

Jon Kabat-Zinn wrote a book, *Mindfulness for All*, which I truly enjoyed. He writes about how unaware we all are of "how the world is treating us" and "how we are treating the world." It's such a decisive time in history for us to realize that these aspects of life are not separate. This naivety is insensitive to the ways our lives shape and impinge on the world and the ways in which the world shapes our lives in a collaborative twist of interdependence and reciprocity. This insensitivity keeps us from the possibilities that could forever benefit our species and our world.

"Coming to our senses is the work of no time at all, only of being present and awake here and now, says Zinn. He calls this *mindfulness*: "the awareness that arises from paying attention on purpose, in the present moment and non-judgmentally. Mindfulness is synonymous with awareness."

Judgment: The Ego's Game

Eckhart Tolle says, "Ego and awareness cannot coexist." When we become aware of the ego in us, it stops being our ego. Whatever happens, it just becomes an old mind pattern that does nothing but bring unwanted feelings from past experiences.

We are all wounded souls who are afraid of love, and we seem to use judgment as a shield to protect ourselves. Does it really protect us? How long does that feeling of self-righteousness last? In reality, it weakens our energy because we are out of alignment with our true nature. Judgment is much more harmful than most are aware of. At the same time, it provides a window into our souls and the reactive buttons we've built by letting the ego tell us we're not special enough or we are more special than others. ACIM explains that judgment does not apply to reality, which is a given, and that we are all *one*. "Reality is only known and accepted, not judged." The correct use of judgment is toward the ego. Here, we can judge that how the ego keeps us separate is untrue and depressing. We can decide to live authentically, and when judgment wants to play its game of rivalry, we can choose to forgive ourselves and others for needing to fight for love, rather than be the love that we literally are.

We all go to great lengths to hide our vulnerability, when, in fact, vulnerability is our most precious healer. Our ability and courage to expose our wounds free us from the ego's games and let us recognize our true nature. They expose our misdirected perceptions and the masks we use to hide the pain and heartbreak that live deep in our subconscious.

Our true nature is love; the ego's game is to keep us from love. Let's now build conscious awareness of the fact that humankind has believed and accepted the ego mind-set as our true selves, which has kept us victim to fear, guilt, shame, and a long list of unwanted feelings and emotions. You're reading this book because you know you want truth in your life and something inside you is telling you to go find it. It's the generation to return to love and heal your misperceptions that have blinded you over time. Believe it or not, love terrifies most of us because we believe that love and pain are indivisible. We must not judge this very detrimental, limiting belief but witness it with love. Our inner children are innocent and waiting to be integrated, to secure a safe place in our hearts, and support our wholeness and integrity. Love heals all.

Gabrielle Bernstein wrote a wonderful book titled *Judgment Detox*. She, too, is a student of ACIM. I recommend this text to many of my coaching clients. She details how to bring to light your fears and untangle the web of your ego and its untruths. Remember to be easy on yourself and not judge your judgments when they come up; just see them as a call for love. The judgment detox is a process, and a very valuable one at that.

Ceaseless Prayer

Even before you ask, scripture says, that which your desire with your heart, has been given unto you. This powerful statement is paramount if we are going to understand the way quantum physics works. Prayer is not just the Our Father or the Hail Mary; it is communication with the Divine

Asking is not begging. It is not an appeal to God for a favor, which he may or may not bestow on you if you're "good" enough. Begging and wanting come from an energy of lack and give you a lack of energy back (cause and effect), rather than the supply that is yours for the asking.

The unlimited universal field of intention contains all possibilities. The way to create things out of this powerful field of pure energy is by attention, intention, and belief. It's also imperative that you practice detachment and trust. You wouldn't dig up a seed to see that it is growing.

When you pray ceaselessly, you intend your desire wholeheartedly, with focus and certainty. You give it to the power of intention and become detached from it. You watch it through faith and belief, with no attachment to how or when it will happen. This is prayer.

Praying without ceasing means going through every day with a focused intention for all your life's desires, with confidence and conviction and, of course, gratitude that they are happening as you envision them. Praying ceaselessly must become a lifestyle. Prayer is meant to be active and part of your general wakefulness. It should be co-creative, not a cry for help in times of need. Be assertive, and intend to receive. "Ask and it will be given unto you; seek and you shall find."

Hopefully, one day, you will realize that even the request is unnecessary; you are one with the Source, including the thing you desire, and you are the grantee and granter of your heart's desires. Your prayers will be genuine gratitude for what is given unto you.

7

The Field of Intention

This is probably the heart of this text—the life source of this study—as intention is the life source of all.

Wayne Dyer, one of my favorite authors, made me aware that intention and its power are far greater than any individual willpower or persistent ego. He commented on Carlos Castaneda's book *The Active Side of Infinity* because two sentences stood out to him. Castaneda wrote, "Intent is a force that exists in the Universe. When sorcerers (those who live *of* the Source) beckon intent, it comes to them and sets up the path to attainment, which means sorcerers always accomplish what they set out to do" and "Intention is not something you do, but a force that exists in the Universe as an invisible field of energy." Castaneda reasoned that the sorcerer could achieve a level of awareness that made available incredible things. He said, "The task of the sorcerer was to face infinity," or *intention*, and the sorcerers immersed themselves in this field daily.

Intention is a force within all of us, and we all have the capability to magnetize this force. Some researchers believe that, rather than our brain's thoughts or modules, our imagination and creativity collaborate with the field of intention.

Lynne McTaggart also wrote a book about the study of the presence of a faster, higher energy dimension, or the power of intention. Her book *The Field: The Quest for the Secret Force of the Universe* supports the idea that we all can tap into and use the field of intention. McTaggart has actually written many books; another one is titled *The Intention Experiment.* Many brilliant authors have written about this field and the energy of manifestation. It really can be a mind-blowing study of life and a demonstration of potentiality.

Everything—yes, everything—has intent built into it. There is *no place* that it's not. We, too, are intended from this energy field. At the moment of conception, life begins, and intention oversees the growth process. Everything about us—our body form, our physical features, and even our death—is all there. I'm sure you're wondering what exactly happens at the moment of conception. When does this life born of intention begin?

Rather than get too scientific, I'll let Einstein describe the conundrum of conception. At our origin, we are formless energy, and in that formless, vibrating energy field, intention abides. Yes, there are molecules, then atoms, then electrons and subatomic particles, and then sub-subatomic particles too. (Einstein, however, discovered that there is no particle at our Source and particles don't create particles.) The miracle of conception is quite a puzzle; however, we do know that this infinite energy field, which is intention, is genuine, unbounded energy vibrating so fast that it defies measurement and is a major player in our inception.

This field of intent really can't be described in words, for words arise from the field, just as the questions do. In this "placeless place" of intention, everything is handled for us. It creates existence, beats our hearts, heals our wounds, and does this for everything and everyone. Intention is an energy that manifests in gazillions of ways in our physical world and all parts of us too, including our soul, body, thoughts, and emotions. It influences everything in the Universe, physical and nonphysical.

The only way we can disband from this powerful force is by believing we're separate from it. Activating the power of intention is a way back to our Source. When we align with this omnipresent power that resides within everything, it highlights the reality that we are absolutely connected by this all-inclusive energy field and the unlimited possibilities of what we'd like to be and what we'd like to do and achieve, in addition to everything in the Universe that will support us.

What has happened to us that we have lost our natural ability to connect? After all, animals and nature don't get disconnected and don't question intention. Humans have seemingly higher brain function and also have formulated a fallacious idea about who and what they are, called the *ego*. It doesn't matter how hard you try; you can't reach intention through the ego.

The ego wants you to believe that you are what you have, and you are what you do or what others think of you. It wants you separate from everyone and all that you believe is missing in your life. The ego and spirit can't exist in peace together; consequently, unworthiness is inevitable. The ego plays this game to keep you dispirited and your energy low. This false self especially wants to estrange you from your true self of passion and love. This treacherous game that the ego plays can literally kill you. It's absolutely the reason for the addiction epidemic in our world today. Let's expose this thief for robbing us of the magnificence of possibility and cocreation. The ego imposes this victim mentality on its prey, which doesn't play out well, after your awareness shines a light on this deceptive villain. Before you learn how to take command of the creative process of your life, rather than being a casualty to the ego's unhealthy regime, let's look at the seven aspects of intention.

Let's begin by understanding that reasoning your way to intention is pointless. Instead, begin to be open to a new and exciting awareness. This silent knowing of intention can inspire you to set aside your rational thought patterns and collaborate with your soul of love, trust, and illumination. After all, *introspection* and *soul-searching* are one of the secrets to achieving joy and fulfillment on this transcendent adventure of *being* and *living*.

Defining the Seven Aspects of Intention

Dr. Wayne Dyer wrote a comprehensive study simplifying this mystifying energy field in his awe-inspiring best seller *The Power of Intention: Learning to Co-Create Your World Your Way*. If you really want to get excited about an all-out investigation into this fascinating, creative energy field, I suggest you scrutinize this book. I'm just summarizing his prodigious work to help you understand this magnificent power's ability to positively influence your potential in a life of choice rather than victimization.

If you could see intention through your REAL-eyes, you'd REALeyes that it is invisible, but it's a super vibration and the Source of everything. The power of intention can't be explained in words, so let's imagine this energy field containing these seven terms that describe the seven aspects of intention: (1) *creativity*, (2) *love*, (3) *kindness*, (4) *beauty*, (5) *expansion*, (6) *unlimited abundance*, and (7) *receptivity*. Furthermore, when you are out of balance and life seems to be working against you, it's advantageous to realize you have disconnected from this power of intention and, more often than not, the ego is playing games with you. So, let's delve deeper into Dyer's seven faces or aspects of intention, as if you were able to remove the shroud that keeps this field from your rational mind and sensory perception.

The Aspect of Creativity

Creativity is the heart of intention. It's the first aspect of this limitless power and the creative demonstration of the capabilities of the intention that created us and created an environment suitable for our vital needs. Nothing would exist if the power of intention weren't creative.

At one time, you were formless energy, then a seed and an embryo, and in the end a physical body. You were brought from *nowhere* to *here now* by this creative energy that contained intention. This life-giving spirit that intends you toward continuous creativity so you create and cocreate whatever you focus your power of intention on, this omnipotent power of creative energy, is a principal part of you. It's a subsidy you have inherited and can direct you toward a life of manifested desires for you and all of humanity.

The Aspect of Love

The aspect of love only wants for you to thrive and grow. So, let's look at emotion and thought as pure energy. When higher energies intermingle with lower energies, lower energies convert to higher energetic vibrations. An example of this is a dark room has lower energy than a well-lit room. When a light turns on in that room, not only does the darkness disappear, but the room wondrously illuminates. The aspect of love can do the same thing, as it has a higher, faster energy than hate, frustration, worry, guilt, and many lower energies. Choose love, and take the time to embody love through your intention and attention. Make it a game of accepting what is and allowing this loving energy of intention, which wants nothing but the best for you, to flow through you.

St. Francis composed a famous prayer appealing to God to make him an instrument of his peace. "Where there is hatred, let me sow love; where there is injury, pardon; where there is doubt, faith," and so on.

He was aiming for our power to dispel hate and transform it to love. Essentially, hatred can be converted into the energy of love, in the presence of love. This applies to you too. You can transform hatred toward others or yourself into the love-granting life force of intention. Ultimately, "love is the most powerful but still the most unknown energy of creation," as Pierre de Chardin says.

The Aspect of Kindness

Surely, if an aspect of intention is love, kindness would also seem a natural feature of a loving energy that intends for what it's creating to flourish. Many studies have proven that directing a simple act of kindness toward another boosts one's immune system. Even more fascinating is that a person observing the act of kindness has similarly favorable results.

This positive effect of kindness can activate more serotonin, the "happy hormone," in the immune systems of both the recipient of the kindness and the person extending the kindness. Serotonin is a natural substance in our bodies that makes us feel more joyful and peaceful. With the rise of depression, our mental health care system uses many antidepressants to trigger serotonin chemically and ease the epidemic of melancholia. The natural remedy of kindness, this simple aspect of intention, could clearly benefit our culture.

The Aspect of Beauty

It's not surprising that beauty is an aspect of intention. The nature of intent infinitely communicates love and beauty, mixed with the other five aspects of this all-pervasive energy.

John Keats, the brilliant poet, wrote, "Beauty is truth, truth beauty, that is all ye know on earth, and all ye need to know." Certainly, truth abides in all creation, so for this reason, as Keats so passionately expounds, *truth and beauty are one.* Knowing this, you can activate beneficial insights into applying intuition and your imagination. By choosing to see beauty in everything and everyone, you become familiar with the creative power within all things in your everyday world, including yourself. Seeing loveliness or beauty, even in the face of the worst conditions, you are able to gaze into the pulchritudinous spirit of intent.

The Aspect of Expansion

Life, in its fundamental nature, continually searches for more and more expression. The principle of increase means it has a continuously expanding energy of progression. Subsequently, an aspect of intention manifests as existence eternally evolving. This absolute power of intention represents itself as the impartial objective of expanding love, kindness, creativity, and beauty. What better way to strengthen your life than to expand and increase all conditions? After all, it's the true nature of intention to be in the position of increased expression; hence, it's true for you too.

I remember my life expanding when I was driving my car one day on vacation in Florida. All of a sudden, I heard a voice in my consciousness repeat, "You are *magnificent*," several times. I was overcome by a feeling of joy like none I'd ever felt before, grander, more wonderful, and more awe-inspiring. Within seconds, I was thinking of my body image and my baby-fine hair, and the feeling dissipated. I remember thinking, *Oh, the ego just slipped into the frame of my thinking in the lower right-hand corner of this somewhat visual image.* The ego was a little bubble. As soon as I noticed the bubble, it seemed to pop, and my image was framed no longer in a small box but in a more expansive space than I'd ever witnessed before. I was extremely excited to have observed such a profound sense of awareness. Life was speaking to me; my spirit had been telling me how *magnificent* I was and am, and suddenly, my human body and ego had come through, limiting my magnificence and consciousness. However, the ego or the bubble popped, and infinity surrounded me again, and the frame disappeared or just enlarged and expanded in space. I had experienced a miracle or, as ACIM states, a change of perception.

Trust this aspect of expansion, and allow the spirited state of increase to reveal itself through you and for you and everyone you meet in your day-to-day encounters. Know that unbounded beneficial consequences are the best possibilities. That way, your life will be less worrisome and even stress-free. In the long run, when we establish our relationship to this aspect of intention, we will expand our lives through this supreme power and take control back from the ego, which was always a detail of intention's intent. To expand our consciousness is our ultimate goal.

The Aspect of Unlimited Abundance

This aspect of intention has absolutely no boundaries, is everywhere at once, and is immeasurably bountiful. This generous gift is what we were created from. Consequently, we, too, can experience this in our lives. It's a gift given freely to you, just as you have air, water, and sun in unlimited supply.

Unfortunately, most of us were taught to think in terms of limited supply. From this limited perspective, our egos have a heyday keeping us from imagining and joyfully experiencing the superabundance that is accessible to all. If we all were created from the power of intention, and it is everywhere, it then enables all things to manifest, to increase, and to supply infinitely.

What a heavenly bequest that we appear to be overlooking, as most of us just exist in a disillusioned way of life. What better way to take pleasure in our lifestyles than by recognizing this limitless abundance and acknowledging our potential as collective beings? After all, these aspects are part of our consciousness when we live in unity with the Source of all life.

The Aspect of Receptivity

The last aspect of intention that we will examine is the receptive side of intention. Simply stated, intention is receptive to all. The truth is that we only need to be willing to recognize it and receive it. In order to harness the receptivity or vibration of intention, we must provide within ourselves a perception equivalent to the essence of the universal mind. Furthermore, it's critical that we are receptive not only to receiving guidance accessible to us so we manifest our mortal intentions, but also to sending this energy back to society.

Reciprocity works for all things. It gives me what I need to flow from Infinite Intelligence and write this book. "By being receptive, I'm in harmony with the power of intention of the universal creative force," says Wayne Dyer. Think about what that simple statement undeniably means.

Reciprocity works in a multitude of ways, lining us up to the right people in our lives, creating miracles in health and strength and whatever we passionately desire. Ultimately, the unbounded potential of this energy field allows all things to materialize, even before we communicate our wishes, as this generous *silent knowing* invariably delivers the strongest energy that's expressed.

Linking to Intention

How do we go about connecting to the Source and accessing this creative principle and its power? We must continually reside in the imaginings of an absolute, infinite power that is producing the results that we desire. An artist provides a good example of this. His or her creations aren't produced by the qualities of the paint or even the canvas. The art would not exist if the artist's thoughts and feelings did not bring about this creative process. It's the artist's creative mind linking with intention that forms an artistic masterpiece. Just as the power of intention longs for a grander expression of life, a true artist longs for a grander expression of his or her thoughts and visions.

Our job is to think about and imagine the energies of life, love, kindness, and beauty, and the creative, unbounded, and receptive spirit of intention. Every action that's in accordance with these activating aspects of intention admits our connection to intention's power.

Once again, we can see how imagination plays an essential part in the production of creative lives. Seeing, feeling, and believing that what we'd like to create is already here, is the image we want to keep close to our heart at all times. Many masters have said this, but I'll say it again: "*Thinking from the end* causes the ones who do this to behave as if all that they'd like to bring about is already and inevitably here."

I want you to focus on your imagination as you read this book and understand that all your goals are a function of your imagery, working and guiding you in the direction that intention had for you even before you manifested. Now, pay close attention because this is an incredibly valuable thought: *What you all are searching for is a vibrational match to your imagined desire and the Source of all creation.*

When imagining, ensure that what you'd like is totally here in the material world. After all, there is no stopping someone who can think from the end. Be unflappable as you use the seven aspects of intention to manifest what you imagine. Dyer parlays his expertise and advises us to write down seven words — (1) *creativity*, (2) *love*, (3) *kindness*, (4) *beauty*, (5) *expansion*, (6) *abundance*, and (7) *receptivity*—and ruminate on the concepts they embody. Be detached from doubt of the outcome. Remember you get what you intend to create when you allow the seven aspects of this creative power to flow through you and to you. That way, you can be in the vibrational vicinity of intent and receptive to its gift of clarity.

You also need to be in receiving mode and to allow this silent knowing to bring an even more vivid, expanded, receptive, abundant, kind, beautiful, loving, and creative possibility to your imagined outcome. Get excited, be elated, think, and feel the love and the deliverance of the realness of this prolific power.

I like very much this quote of Michelangelo's: "The greatest danger for most of us is not that our aim is too high and we miss it, but that it's too low and we reach it."

Another of my favorite messages comes from Jesus of Nazareth: "If you bring forth what is inside you, what you bring forth will save you. If you don't bring forth what is inside you, what you don't bring forth will destroy you."

The power of intention is what's inside us and ready, willing, and able to be brought forth to be of service. We just have to be in vibrational harmony with our true essence. We need to have focus, commitment, and determination to be continually conscious of feeling good, as within the seven aspects of intention, and know this is our key to becoming all we are profoundly capable of being. Imagining this feel-good consciousness is the answer to our prayers.

In his book *Power vs. Force*, David Hawkins writes, "Genius is by definition a style of consciousness characterized by the ability to access high-energy attractor patterns. It is not something that a person *has* nor even something that someone *is*. Those in whom we recognize genius commonly disclaim it. A universal characteristic of genius is humility. The genius has always attributed his insights to some higher influence."

Genius means connecting to the Source in such an energetically consummate way that your ego is consciously diminished.

Take time to find solace in silence, simplify your life, let go of resistance, practice humility, expand your reality, and trust your inner voice and insights. These are just a few of the undertakings that will pave the way to a consistent connection with the field of intention. Begin to cultivate your inner dialogue so it reflects such certainty as to generate highly vibrational, energetic feelings that create an inner belief that the universal Source provides everything and is available to all at any time in our spiritual journey.

8

The Laws of the Universe

I'm pretty sure most of us have at some point felt that there has to be more to life than just our day-to-day existence. We think, *there has to be something more, but what is it?* Well, the laws of the Universe reveal the answer to this question. These undeniable laws control all things without ambivalence. They determine the world around us, as well as our inner beings. These principles are not open for negotiation.

The real question is *Why aren't we taught these Universal Laws during our schooling or training as human beings living on this magnetic planet, Earth?* Are they hidden from us, as surely no one talks about them? Many believe that those in authority are just afraid of the irrefutable power of this information that could revolutionize our mere existence.

It is our personal responsibility to learn as much as we can about these laws, so as to transform our capabilities and empower people to use these natural, God-given endowments so they can better their lives and the lives of all humankind.

"As without, so within." Our outer world reflects our inner world. These Universal Laws are our human spirit guidelines that can help us expand our consciousness to accomplish great things, as was always intended. Anything that we want to realize can be found in the secrets of the Universe. They are the key to *all* life, and it's our birthright to learn the omnipotent capabilities of these commandments and use them to better our world and serve to teach and demonstrate them to others.

Seven Laws of Hermetic Philosophy

According to *The Kybalion*, "The Principles of Truth are Seven; he who knows these, understandingly, possesses the Magic Key before whose touch all Doors of the Temple fly open."

The Kybalion says, "Hermetic philosophy, originally published in 1908 by a person or persons under the pseudonym of 'The Three Initiates,' is a book claiming to be the teachings of Hermes Trismegistus." He authored a series of sacred texts based on Hermeticism (connected to the founder of alchemy and astrology).

The Law of Mentalism

The All is mind. The Universe is mental. The All, or the material Universe, and all with matter and energy, all that is perceptible to our material senses, is the Spirit, or a universal, infinite, living mind. The Universe is simply a mental creation of the All.

An understanding of the law of mentalism allows an individual to grasp the idea of the mental Universe, and to utilize that for his or her advancement and well-being. It is written, "He who grasps the truth of the Mental Nature of the Universe is well advanced on the Path to Mastery."

The Law of Correspondence

"As above, so below; as below, so above."

This law explains the truth that the laws and the various planes of being and life always correspond. There are planes beyond our knowing, and this principle is of universal execution and manifestation

on the various planes of the material, mental, and spiritual Universe—
it is Universal Law. Knowledge of the law of correspondence allows
humankind to reason intelligently from the known to the unknown.
In the material world, physics explains that vibration, energy, motion,
and light have their corresponding principles in the etheric Universe.

An easier and more useful way to understand this law is "As within,
so without." You see, your outer world of consciousness reflects your
inner world of consciousness. I believe this to be a gift of life. We see
within because of this law. We can see what is actually working in our
lives and what is not working in our lives in order to make changes
and learn and grow. Life shows us what our predominant energy is,
as reflected in our daily lives, but are we paying attention? Do we
appreciate this bonus we've been given and adjust without judgment to
a more beneficial setting in our energetic model?

The Law of Vibration

Also known as the *law of attraction* or the *law of manifestation*, this
law says, "Nothing rests; everything moves; everything vibrates."

This law explains the contrast between different manifestations of
matter, mind, energy, and spirit originate from diverse rates of vibration.
The vibration of the spirit seems almost motionless, as it vibrates at a
staggering rate of velocity and intensity. There are gazillions of varying
degrees of vibration. Everything has its own vibrational frequency,
unique unto itself. The Universe moves, vibrates, and travels in circular
patterns, and the same principles in the material world work in the
etheric world. "Like attracts like" is an easy way to make sense of this
indiscriminate law.

A conscious understanding of this law allows us to control our and
others' mental vibrations, if studied in depth. One of the old writers
was quoted as saying, "He who understands the Principles of Vibration
has grasped the scepter of Power."

Basically, since everything is constantly vibrating, this law works
side by side with the law of attraction, as we are always attracting

the vibration that we send out. The law of attraction and the law of vibration go hand in hand to manifest the highest or lowest vibration emanating from our most focused thoughts and feelings.

The Law of Polarity

"Everything is dual; everything has poles; everything has its pair of opposites; like and unlike are the same; opposites are identical in nature, but different in degree; extremes see; all truths are but half-truths; all paradoxes may be reconciled" are the same, as described by Hermetic philosophy.

For example, this law explains that heat and cold are the varying degrees of the same thing. Light and dark, small and large, and noisy and quiet are the same, as explained by the law of polarity. Everything is and isn't at the parallel time; there are two sides to everything. Everything has two poles, with varying degrees separating them.

The Hermetic masters believed they could convert evil to good by understanding this law and devoting time and study to the law of polarity.

A basic understanding of the law says everything is on a continuum and has a contrasting counterpart. By using this law, we can change undesirable thought energy and vibration by concentrating or focusing on more desirable thoughts.

The Law of Rhythm

"Everything flows out and in; everything has its tides; all things rise and fall; the pendulum-swing manifests in everything; the measure of the swing to the right is the measure of the swing to the left; rhythm compensates."

Everything in our world vibrates and progresses to certain rhythms. "These rhythms determine cycles, seasons, patterns and stages of development." God's Universe expresses the regularity of each cycle.

This law plainly defines the truth that in *everything*, there is evidence of a measured motion, to and FRO. The tide flows in, and the tide flows out. If you have ever witnessed, while swimming, the ebb and flow of a strong tide, you know that your best bet is to relax and go with the flow, and you will actually enjoy the rhythm. If instead you panic and try to swim against the tide, you'll be in for the fight of your life. The ocean has many great lessons about the rhythms of life.

It's important to acknowledge a current, progression, or movement when you're fighting against the natural rhythm, no matter if it's in your personal or business life. Just think about how in relationships, one minute, things are just great, and the next, you're asking yourself, "What the heck just happened?" How about in your job? Things are going so well, and then you get a phone call, and the deal is no longer happening—oh boy. These are the times when things seem out of rhythm or they have an awkward or uneasy rhythm. Remember, what we resist persists, so try to go with the flow. Sometimes, blind faith—or my favorite, *trust life*—is the default emotion I like to turn to.

The Law of Causes and Effect

This is also known as *karma*. "Every Cause has its Effect; every Effect has its Cause; everything happens according to Law; Chance is but a name for Law not recognized; there are many planes of causation, but nothing escapes the Law."

Nothing just happens; it happens according to the law. The masses are brought along by the law, obeying their environment and the wishes of others, whereby the masters rise above the plane and dominate their moods and qualities as well as the environment and become movers, rather than pawns. The masters use the law, instead of being its tool.

Every action, including every thought, has a reaction. "We reap what we sow."

Basically, everything happens for a reason, as every cause has an effect. The law states that all attainment, happiness, wealth, and success result from specific causes. This indicates that if we can be clear about the *effect* of what we want, most likely, we'll achieve it. The best way to accomplish this is to study others who have achieved the same intention, and by doing what they did, we, too, can cause the effect to have the same outcome.

"Your rewards in life will always be equal to the amount and quality of service rendered, in the long run," as Denise Waitley says.

The Law of Gender

"Gender is in everything; everything has its Masculine and Feminine Principles; Gender manifests on all planes."

The law of gender on the physical plane is *sex*; on the higher planes, it takes a higher form, but the principle remains the same. Every male form has a female form, and every female form has a male form, which is essential for life to exist. This law governs what we understand as creation.

In a perfect world, let's say two people are in a conversation; one is speaking, and one is listening. When the one speaking stops and listens to the one who was listening, the roles reverse, and let's just say that out of this exchange, new ideas or plans form from these corresponding energies. This dialogue, between the giving and taking, gives rise to a new creation.

In reality, we incorrectly use the word *creation*, as all new things are the end product of something that was changing into something that now is.

Bob Proctor says, "Without the male and female gender in all things, there would not be a difference of potential perpetuation of motion, nor a regeneration. This is in truth the creative Law. The law decrees that everything in nature is both male and female. Both are required for life to exist."

The Remaining Five Immutable Laws of the Universe (Totaling Twelve Laws of the Universe)

The Law of Gestation

The Hermetic laws don't include the law of gestation within their *Kybalion*. I know that we now link the two together when studying quantum physics and the Universal Laws with their irrefutable principles.

This law is the *creative law*. It commands that everything in nature is both male and female. It also stipulates that all seeds, even seeds of thought, have a gestation period before they are evidenced. The time it takes for a seed to grow to maturity and material form is referred to as the *gestation period*.

It's our job to select the right seeds, or the right thoughts and feelings, and get into the right vibration by focusing repeatedly on those feel-good thoughts. Then we must trust the Universe does its handiwork to engender our heart's desire.

The Law of Action

A simple explanation is that this law must be practiced for things to be evidenced on this earth. We must undertake actions that support our thoughts, emotions, words, and visions. We must do things that will help achieve the results we aspire to. If we don't take actions that align with our thoughts and desires, we have no hope of getting the results we are aiming for.

We have preciously read about the law of attraction, where we learned about focusing on our most valued desires. It also mentioned that we should not worry about *how*. You were told to trust the Universe. This is where the law of action comes into play. In most instances, you will know when to take action, but don't concentrate on what way this will happen. Just rest assured and listen, and you'll know what to do.

When given a direction, you must *act* in a way that supports your desire. The archenemies of this law are fear and laziness, so do not let them get in the way of the law of action.

This law is very similar to the law of cause and effect. The action is the cause, and that action always has a corresponding effect. If you take even a small action, like making a to-do list every morning or reading books, it will set in motion proportionate effects and change your actual future. If you can create a daily habit, which takes approximately twenty-one days, then it can magnify your results.

The Law of Compensation

Again, this law echoes the law of cause and effect, or "What you reap, you sow." Ralph Waldo Emerson wrote an essay on compensation and in it states, "Each person is compensated in the like manner for which he or she has contributed." Another way to explain this is that we are never compensated for more than we put in.

This law can also show us how those who make it a practice to put more in than they take out (overcompensation) are often rewarded with great success. These people do more than they are paid for but are usually over-rewarded with their colleagues' respect and the financial rewards that accompany personal prosperity.

If we infuse our mind with feelings, thoughts, and visions of good fortune and happiness, we will be compensated for those affirmative, supportive impressions in our everyday life. Our mental perspective and our feelings of gratitude and fulfillment are also templates of information that we have put in our mind and will support the compensation process. This law, like all the laws, is constant and indiscriminate. The gifts of compensation are given to us through the visible effects of our actions and accomplishments in money, relationships, blessings, and endowments.

The Law of Perpetual Transmutation of Energy

Perpetual transmutation means that energy unceasingly moves into and out of different forms, never created nor destroyed. Nothing is constant or remains the same.

We all have the power to change the conditions of our lives within us. It is true that higher vibrations consume and transform lower vibrations to such a degree that each of us can alter the energies in our lives by understanding the Universal Laws and applying these concepts. Just like that, it can result in miraculous changes.

Our thoughts are considered the most commanding form of energy that permeates all time and space in our Universe. They have the intrinsic likelihood to morph from nonphysical to physical in all respects.

Think about how the sun's rays shine on the vegetables we eat. Energy is then stored in the vegetables' molecules, and that energy is passed on to us when we eat the vegetables. We can then use this energy as metabolic energy, needed for our own liveliness. Some energy is visible, and some is invisible; different forms of energy are affecting every molecule of our bodies, through the surrounding air we breathe, etc..

The Law of Relativity

Basically, everything is relative. It's difficult to define something unless we compare it to something else. Until we compare the thing in question to something else, we cannot answer; your home is small or large compared to a studio apartment or a mansion. So, your past experiences influence your judgments. But actually, everything *just is*. Let's remember it's all about perception, as we learned earlier.

It's therefore useful to keep this law in mind when we see something or someone as "more" than what we have or can become. It's important that we not compare ourselves to others and we waive judgment and such comparisons at times like these. Everything is relative. Bear in mind *it just is*.

Each of us will receive lessons to these questions and challenges, tests, or limitations, so to speak. These challenges will strengthen the light within each of us and the connections to our hearts as we take action to solve these tests or limitations. They will also teach us to not compare our challenges to others' challenges and to put them in proper perspective, for, you see, no matter how bad you think your situation is, someone is always in a worse place. It's all relative.

9

Mindfulness

Mindfulness is one of the most fundamental skills known to humanity. However, this elementary capability, which is part of our birthright, has somehow gotten lost in our high-speed world. Mindfulness is a way of being and a function of moment-to-moment awareness or consciousness. The good news is that we can relearn how to be present or in the moment by teaching ourselves simple exercises. For example, we can meditate and use the breath as our focus, or mindfully take a walk, or use mindfulness in any simple daily activity. These different methods can bring about a natural awareness over time and make living more intimate.

The actual practice of mindfulness goes back thousands of years. Buddhist philosophers took great interest in how the mind works and how to discipline the mind to be more present. They gave mindfulness a central role in their teaching. Current mindfulness training systems come mainly from the Buddhist method of meditation. Most of us are familiar with the Dalai Lama, a very influential Buddhist teacher and spiritual leader of Tibet. Of course, we don't have to be Buddhist, or religious, to practice mindfulness.

To give you a little background, mindfulness training became popular in our Western culture in the 1970s. In 1979, Jon Kabat-Zinn, the author, who I mentioned earlier, was also a professor of medicine and created the Stress Reduction Clinic and the Center for Mindfulness in Medicine, Health Care, and Society at the University of Massachusetts Medical School. Today, many medical centers and hospitals offer the stress reduction program that Kabat-Zinn created, the mindfulness-based stress reduction (MBSR) course. This eight-week course trains candidates to be mindful and relate to stress and pain in a better way than through overwhelm and reaction.

Today, research in the science and medical communities is extensively investigating mindfulness and the enormous benefits of mindful practices. Physical health and mental health along with plain old well-being can profit from this awareness.

Mindful meditation will not, however, take us to an altered state. It is a place where we already are right now. It's a place to breathe into the moment. Thoughts will not necessarily disappear when in a mindful meditative state, so we should allow them to flow and gently return ourselves to a consistent focus, which is usually the breath. Experiencing random thoughts is like watching a cloud moving through the sky. Thoughts are just *thoughts*, the definition of which is ideas, opinions, views, and impressions. Facts, they are not.

Mindfulness comes into being when we give up sleepwalking through life. In actuality, we are ruminating in unpleasant thoughts of the past or fears of the future—most of the time, anyway. It's exhausting, this autopilot chatter in our heads, and we wonder why stress and overwhelm are chronic conditions in this day and age.

To raise our mindfulness, we can first acknowledge that we are on autopilot and breathe into the experience of the present moment. We can begin by paying attention to what is going on in our body, in our mind, or in our environment. When we ground ourselves in mindfulness, we can also become more aware of the habits that make us unhappy or stressed, which we want to replace with new choices. This consistent practice of awareness can be as simple as clicking an off switch and allowing a new portal to our mental and visual outlook.

Mindfulness, or moment-to-moment consciousness, can teach us to be more aware of our bodies and the stress signals they use to give us the opportunity to respond more effectively. This way, we do not have to be as reactive, and we can have a more balanced response to a seemingly stressful situation. We can then take intelligent action and ease the unreasonable emotional states of losing our temper and overdoing it, and whatever else we do to alleviate the discomfort of stress response.

Most people think that mindfulness is only about the mind, but one of the core focuses is the body. Mindfulness means relearning how to be fully inside our bodies, to be *embodied*. When we are fully aware of our bodies, our minds and bodies are synched. We become whole and connected. This way, we feel the body from the inside and listen to the messages it sends us. After all, our bodies register all our experiences, good or bad. Very often, we are unaware of how the body is registering the stories of our lives. I, for one, grind my teeth at night and wear a mouth guard so I don't do extensive damage.

It's important to pay attention to our bodies and connect with our experiences through our senses. Rather than just *think* about them, we need to come back to the *being*. When we become more aware of our emotions and physical sensations, we'll discover that they are not that difficult to handle, and we won't have to repress them and act them out. Coming home to our bodies, a place we can trust, and feeling its natural stability and comfort is worth the effort for both our physical and mental health.

Although mindfulness helps us open ourselves up to wider possibilities, the journey may take us in unexpected directions. This practice is not a quick fix and is not meant to have constant expectation and judgment, as it may not always have consistent results. The work here is more about accepting who we are *right now*, rather than looking for big changes.

The way we create mindfulness is as individual as the day is long. We can have conventional meditation sessions where we set aside time for practice, which can vary from five minutes' time to long retreat sessions. We can even do it in the blink of an eye. Yes, we can pause at any moment in our busy lives and notice *where we are*.

Please do not misunderstand me. The practice of pausing is not meant to replace formal meditation; the two-go hand in hand. In meditation, we take ourselves out of our normal activities and expand our ability to be present and connect with a powerful, magnificent sense of spaciousness. And, as we train our minds to meditate, we also let this pervade our daily lives through frequent little pauses throughout the day. Train yourself to pick something that reminds you to pause. It could be a sound you hear on your phone or an activity as simple as having a drink of water. Decide that each time you hear or taste or do this thing, you will pause for a few seconds and notice what you are doing and where you are. Take a few deep breaths, and then move on.

The Breath

The breath is the most basic of all human functions, and *breath* is Latin for "spirit." We need nothing special to be aware of the breath. Let's just say that when we are aware of our breath, it is *this* breath, in *this* moment. It is not yesterday's breath or tomorrow's breath but a true connection to the present moment. When we tune in to our breath, our bodies and minds are in sync. A wonderful exercise I've learned to do is to use my conscious awareness of my breath as a haven, and when I get caught up in stressful or anxious thoughts, I just breathe, with all my attention on my breath. I tune in to the physical sensation of breathing, not thinking about it but just *being* with it. You will find your mind wandering from the breath, but that's not a problem. The mind naturally wanders, and no matter how many times it wanders, just lovingly and gently bring it back to the breath. Let it breathe itself. Be inquisitive about the breath. Feel your body, your lungs, your temperature and strength, the depth of your breath and so on.

The Body

Mindfulness is about the mind, and yes, learning about the paradigms within the mind is an important piece of the process. We learned earlier that a core premise of mindfulness is relearning how to be fully inside your body. The physical body has a magical way of securing you in the present moment. Amazingly enough, when you are conscious of your body, your mind and body are in sync, and you are connected or whole.

Everything we experience in this lifetime—the incidents we like and the ones we don't like—registers in our bodies. We can feel it, but are we aware? Our bodies are constantly releasing and opening, softening and closing, bracing and clenching. When we begin to grow more aware of our bodies, we will notice how our thoughts and emotions are linked to our bodily sensations. Not only stress but anger, frustration, desire, and joy play their roles in our bodies' physiology. By learning to allow our feelings, including the tough ones, in our bodies, we can respond to our experiences in a healthy way, rather than just falling victim to habitual patterns or paradigms.

The next time you experience anything uncomfortable, try to connect through the senses; rather than *thinking* about it, try the *being* approach. You'll begin to see that you can handle even the difficult situations and you don't have to react to them or repress them. Once you've rediscovered the body as a home base, a place you can trust, you'll begin to feel its natural, grounded, and stable qualities.

Responding Rather Than Reacting

We are constantly reacting to our experiences. Let's remember what we learned earlier—that *reaction* is generally rooted in the past, and *response* is generally happening in the now. We also have three fundamental responses: (1) like, (2) dislike, and (3) indifference. These instinctive reactions are so habitual that we don't even notice them, although they dictate how we filter our life experiences. Understanding and relearning that we can freshly, directly experience life through our senses can, in fact, make us more accurately aware of life's beauty and its gifts.

In mindfulness, we can *turn away* from our natural reactions and instead *turn toward* them. We can allow ourselves to be with (notice I said not *in* but *with*) this uncomfortable energy, the adrenaline, and the tension. Oddly enough, as we do this, the energy of our anger, panic, or overwhelm can exist and then move *through* us. This is quite obviously a less destructive response than resisting or burying our emotional reaction, and it gives us more choice in what happens next. A response is more readily available than a reaction when we lovingly allow a moment of mindful awareness into our consciousness. It's as simple as a pause and a breath.

Thoughts

Thoughts are not a problem in mindfulness. We can learn quite a bit from them, actually. An empty mind is not our goal. You see, thoughts are as normal as a wave in the ocean. But let's be clear; our thoughts and ourselves are *not* the same thing. As we learn to meditate and be mindful, we can begin to see that thoughts are not solid. We can begin to let go of them and lighten their hold on us.

Each time our minds wander off, we can bring them back to our focus, our breath, or our bodies, whatever we choose. It's important not to judge our thoughts as good or bad; it's all just thinking. Try not to analyze your thinking or thoughts; just take yourself back to the moment and the focus.

I'm sure most of us have had times when we had a chain reaction of negative thoughts that snowballed into deep worries or fears. We should see these usually subconscious thoughts for what they really are—untruths that are buried deep in our pasts and have run our lives, creating unhealthy habits and imbalances in our bodies. Being mindful can help us interrupt these unhealthy behaviors and create a more beneficial response.

By challenging ourselves with alternative methods of mindfulness, we can find more stability within our day-to-day experiences—a way to love ourselves more or, as I like to say, love ourselves *enough*. Can we love ourselves enough to take the time to change something that hasn't been working and have more time for the "big" mind, or the universal mind, and less time for the chattering in the "small" mind?

Meditation

When we think of meditation, I'm pretty sure most of us don't get too excited about scheduling this challenging practice. Yes, it is a challenge, but possibilities abound within any meditation method. The longing for peace and unity and the need for more human compassion has become a worldwide movement. I'm here to tell you that meditation can be the key to developing more connections, more awareness, and more understanding of the experience of life as we know it.

Let's look at the human mind and its natural recklessness, undisciplined and quite wild model. As we learned earlier, we are experiential beings, here to experience life's ups and downs, joys and sorrows. Life is a verifiable paradox of yes's and no's, good times and bad times, which makes the journey seem tumultuous. Well, some may argue that's what makes life so wondrous, and it's also why it takes us on such a crazy journey. It's training our minds through meditation to be more accepting, kind, and open to the wild ride of our experience that makes life more enjoyable. If we can be more compassionate with life's difficulties and the mind's unpredictability, we can become more comfortable with whatever creation hands us.

Meditation is one of the most productive ways to work with the mind, opening ourselves up to each and every moment in its purest form and entirety. Through it, we can learn to leave behind our false security of thinking through all the events and to-do lists of our lives that creates a false impression of grounded security. We must realize that only the *nowness* of this moment, and then that moment and then another new moment, is the real catalyst for metamorphosis. No moment is like any other moment; each is unique, with unlimited potential and power. Meditation can teach us how to deal with life directly, instant to instant, free from concepts concealed by self-deception and past memories.

If we were to look at the teachings of the Buddha or *Dharma*, who schools us in accepting *the truth of what is,* we'd understand that meditation is intended to remove a lot of self-imposed suffering. He said quite frankly, "I teach only one thing: suffering and the cessation of suffering." The Buddha's principles are about removing not only suffering's symptoms but also its causes. You see, the mind is the root of all suffering and all happiness. The Buddha believed that if we work with our mind, we can relieve the suffering that appears to come from the outside. He taught that when a situation, a person, or even a physical pain challenges us, we must work with our minds through meditation. He viewed this as the only way we'll begin to be at peace in the world we live in.

When the Buddha spoke of suffering, he used the word *dukkha*, which has a different meaning than *pain*. Pain and pleasure are part of our life experience in this world. They are inescapable parts of human life. He said that "pain is" and you just have to accept it as part of life. The word *dukkha* can also mean "never satisfied." As physical beings, we are consistently dissatisfied with the fact that life is both pleasant and unpleasant. This is, in fact, the reality of the human condition. Humans have a strong tendency to want only pleasant, comfortable, or agreeable feelings. We can become very annoyed at any discomfort and will likely run away from it or avoid it altogether.

Just as the weather continually changes our moods and feelings, our internal weather shifts and changes every day. We need not identify with these energies and let them take us down. When something or someone or even physical pain is bothering us, we must begin to work with our minds through meditation.

The Why of Meditation

Meditation opens us up with compassion to whatever is going on. It is not a practice for feeling good or feeling bad. The ideal meditative space we can open up to is forever expansive and can oblige anything that happens to come up. So, you see, the nature of meditation is the training to stay with yourself no matter what thoughts or feelings you think you hear or feel. Subconsciously, we seem to desire a life of only successes. We appear to be unaware of our fear of failure, which is a critical part of evolutionary growth. No judgment is necessary, as it will only continually dissatisfy us, and again, we'll suffer.

At times, meditation can seem very difficult, boring, or extremely uncomfortable, as your back may hurt or your mind may go a million miles a minute. What I'm trying to teach you is a compassionate openness with yourself, your mind, and your life's various situations. This mindful practice of being with yourself and whatever comes your way in the moment is key to living your best life. Meditation can build a consistent dedication and steady loyalty to oneself if done regularly and committedly. It's all about opening the mind and the heart to the joys and the challenges of *what is*, without judgment or labels. As you learn this steadfastness, you learn to be more available to life as it is. You can more easily catch yourself when you react neurotically, close down, or even spin out of control. As you practice staying in meditation, focusing, and always coming back to the breath with gentle, loving kindness for whatever arises, you actually become less subjective and develop a sense of clarity of just seeing and being. When thoughts and feelings come, you can see them clearly. The veil of the past and your habitual patterns and defense mechanisms reveal themselves over time, and you can develop more true understanding and unconditional love for yourself.

Sometimes, in meditation, you may feel emotionally distressed. It's very important to stay with this perceived pain and witness what arises without apprehension. It's not a bad meditation session or a good one when you feel this distress; it just is what it is—an ability to be there for yourself and your ups and downs and ins and outs. Life can surely be sweet or sour. Meditation and its introspective vision can be transformative, exposing your humanness. The more you practice, the more you expose your true self and an unbiased understanding of what's possible. It loosens up the way you hold yourself together and perpetuate your suffering. In truth, our species is just not comfortable with the shifting, ephemeral energy of reality.

You remember we learned that what we resist persists. We seem to innately resist being here now, as it doesn't have any definite commonality. It's the ghost in the closet; it's the *unknown*. By developing our meditation practices, we train ourselves to be attentive to the moment, the thought, the feeling, and especially the unknown. A very important by-product arises as we do this work, and that is courage, which is essential in living a life worth living and having any kind of self-confidence. That place of accepting the unknown or the present moment is an extremely powerful place to the people who aspire to awaken and open their minds and hearts. The present moment is the engine of our meditation and "the fuel for our personal journey," as Pema Chodron, the American-born Buddhist nun, so creatively states. If you want to know more about a simple but powerful type of meditation, I suggest that you read her book *How to Meditate.*

Meditation practices have many different levels. When studying the advanced practices, we can experience other planes of light and dimension, but we must master relaxing in the first level before we can go to another. Once we begin to master these frequencies, we can then move by will to the next level. In each and every level of frequency, we can find what is useful to our further development. These levels are infinite, and if you're a spiritual person, then you know that heaven surrounds us. When this limitless, all-encompassing energy field surrounds us, we learn to cease talking and asking for our needs to be met, as that wish is already known and can be on its way with the correct alignment of emotional vibration. Our quest is to relax, simply listen by emptying our thoughts, and calmly allow the experience of this energy to take us to the higher levels of universal, divine vibration. In this stillness, we can allow divine inspiration to approach us. Once there, we can experience the feeling of oneness, magnificence, and perfect love and *know* that this energy is always there. It's this experience that will radiate off us in this dimension, sharing our light with all we touch.

10

Our Stories

It was the Italian astronomer, physicist, and engineer Galileo who said, "You cannot teach a man anything. You can only help him discover it within himself."

We are all unique in our own way. Each of us has our own potential in this life we've been given on planet Earth. Let it be said that achievement is not the only measure of success; authenticity is the true measure of a life well lived. Trustworthiness, reliability, responsiveness, genuineness, and credibility are the values of an authentic individual. The true essence of our being is pure and loving, and anything less than authenticity will not bring the heart and soul true joy or happiness. Only a false sense of achievement will be the veritable prize, not an accurate sense of the copious rewards of a life lived authentically.

We all have our individual stories; they are as unique as our fingerprints, but are they really accurate? Do we really see the gifts of life and growth in our stories of our past, or are they just a drama we perpetuate to fill a void in our human psyche? Are your stories the grounding foundation of your personality, or are they the *you* you've been dealt, without any options available?

We learned earlier that our beliefs guide our lives and that beliefs are not necessarily facts or truths—more like skewed perceptions or opinions than verifiable truths. Our story lines are what we tell ourselves and each other to excuse ourselves for being apparent victims and not realizing our power to shift our paradigms and create a life on purpose.

Why has no one taught us that our focus is our greatest asset? The laws of nature state that whatever we think about and focus our attention on is indiscriminately created, and not by a loving master nor a devious one but by our energy. Why do we keep defending the lies we've told ourselves for so long, most of which we created from feelings twisted by a misunderstood energy? We shelter our pain in our hearts as a badge of courage rather than as a place to heal the parts of ourselves that we've disowned due to the stories we tell ourselves every day. Why is it we'd rather live with the shadows of the past than love ourselves enough to understand that life's dynamic energy is benevolent and passionate? It doesn't mean to harm us but has gifted us the art of creation through thought, feeling, and focus. What a magnanimous endowment we have been given. Life itself wants nothing more than for us to flourish and realize that we are all one, cocreating within a magnificently diverse Universe.

Life, the Universe, the Source, Divinity, or God loves us more than we can imagine and we can aim not just to feel that but to love it back, shining a light on all we see so more of us can experience joy and passion. Remember we are here for the experience. Service is also an expression of giving back that love, mirroring our authentic nature. We are all lovable; it's innate in our spiritual DNA. *But* do we believe it? Was it affirmed and mirrored consistently when we were children, after being exposed to our world, full of people who didn't believe it, including our parents? The answer is probably *no* in most cases, and this is not a blame game. It's a sad truth because of the unawareness of most of the population. A large number of our parents didn't teach it because they didn't feel lovable, because their parents mirrored unlovable-ness, so they couldn't teach what they didn't know. We also could have experienced peer pressure when we were of school age, and we could have taken the energy of outside influences to heart and mirrored inferiority by being exposed to a myriad of external energies.

Self-judgment and the myth of inadequacy have ruled our lives and fabricated a plethora of negative self-talk, like, "I am not _____" (fill in the blank). Here, I'll help you out: "I am not good enough." "I am not smart enough." "I am not lucky enough." "I am not like anyone else." And on and on it goes. It's time now to tell the true story of our magnificence as spirits with the most magnanimous hearts and souls in creation.

The basic angst of not being lovable is a very damaging impression. It's our "story" from deep within that follows us everywhere, infecting our energy in the life source. It's time to change our stories. Don't misunderstand me, please. Our stories have gotten us to this point, and that's a good thing. Remember life loves us and has always had our best interests at heart.

Let's drop the story line long enough to feel and identify the feelings under our story line. I use this exercise when I feel panicked or anxious in my human experience on this planet. Remember, energy is always changing and never static—as within, so without. I close my eyes and try to sit with the feeling, the dynamic energy of life, the yin and yang of the life source. Yes, it can be painful and uncomfortable, but feeling it without the story line, it's not as life-threatening and devastating. We can begin to see it as just part of universal dynamism. Be courageously present with the energy, and you will begin to understand how dynamic energy works.

Life treats us the way we treat ourselves. You see, my friend, our stories are outdated and misrepresented. Louise Hay and her infamous *mirror work* helped me see the reality of what I am talking about. The basic premise of this work is to look into a mirror every day and tell yourself, "I love you," over and over. I did this practice with a client for support recently. As I looked into the mirror I immediately saw everything wrong with my facial features, oh this eye seems smaller than the other eye and my smile is crooked… I then paused and thought, *this is very telling.* I shook my head and tried again to see *me* and not my body. Wow! I remember emotion overwhelming me, and I cried like I never had before. It felt like I saw myself for the first time, and the sadness of abandonment poured out of me. It was a very powerful exercise. It became very apparent that my work here was to forgive myself for not being cognizant of myself for most of my life. Can we really expect to be loved by life or anyone when we can't see, never mind love, ourselves?

The time has come for us to be the storytellers of the life fully lived, the life of choice, and the life we were meant to create. When people I meet begin to talk their stories *at* me, I consistently tell them, "Tell a different story!"

It's time to tell a different story. Tell the story of what you want rather than the story of what is or what you don't want. Have you ever noticed that if you ask someone what they want, they're more likely to first tell you what they don't want? Unfortunately, most of us have spent so much time thinking about what we don't want that we have no idea what we do want. Let's be sensitive to what's working in our lives and appreciate the positive. Let's take responsibility for what's before us and know that whatever manifests is for our benefit. It's not good, it's not bad—it just *is*. And if you take to heart what you've read in all these pages, you'll essentially become kinder and more loving to yourself and to all of humanity. We can educate ourselves, to learn what works and what doesn't. More importantly, we have a choice to feel good as we adjust the energy of littleness and suffering, of less than, and of unloving and begin to wrap ourselves in the affirmative, supportive arms of Source.

Spend time visualizing, feeling, tasting, and smelling your actual dreams and desires coming true, the fabulous feeling of joy! Feel good, and do this often, as the Universe has to respond to it. Trust the outcome with a grateful heart. Appreciate the old story, the new story, and the life force's momentum and oscillating nature.

We see things not as they are but as *we* are; the world is our mirror. Our life experiences consistently reveal to us what we are emulating through our thoughts and feelings. Our energetic vibration, conscious or unconscious, guides us to see what is working and what is not working. The world we see before us is *all for us and about us*, so see the things we attract, either to heal us, to indulge in, to teach us some life lesson, or to mirror where we are in our relationships, work, love lives, and so on.

As my queries shifted from outside of me to inside of me, my judgements of others and their influence in my life shifted dramatically, and I was able to take responsibility for what was demonstrated in my life and around me. Yes, this changed my outlook very dynamically, as I began to realize, it's all for my benefit.

We are experiential beings, living and learning the truths of our human nature. When we can see the good in the good and the good in the not so good, we demonstrate trust in our loving Source and return to our heart's wisdom. We can heal our perceptions of the past, to create incredible possibility in the future. Now is the time for us to appreciate our natural inheritance as co-creators and re-claim our extraordinary power in order to change ourselves and the world we live in. Today as I enjoy my commitment to my spiritual practices, my natural guidance system navigates me to adjust and recalibrate my emotional balance to see, think, and feel better and better through my life lessons—and even feel really good! For life is a precious gift to be fully lived, enjoyed and appreciated. … After all, "It's All Good."

Epilogue

March 30, 2016, profoundly changed my life. At about 12:00 AM, a loud knocking on my front door woke me up. I was startled but alert as I answered the door and found two Westwood policemen standing in the dark. One of the men solemnly handed me a note and said, "Your son was in an accident, and his heart stopped; that's all we know. A nurse from Brigham and Women's Hospital called us, and she wants you to call her. Here is her phone number." I vaguely remember asking the policemen questions before they said they had no other information and walked away. I was in absolute panic and shock. I called my youngest son who also lived in Boston and my son and daughters in California but couldn't do much more. Oddly enough, what I do remember is driving ever so slowly. I can't tell you why I remember going so slowly except that I've never felt more shaken and vacant than that night. I kept trying to call the nurse as I drove, but the phone kept falling out of my hand. Finally, I reached her, and she said nothing more than what the officers had told me and that the doctors would be waiting for me with more information. I desperately wanted to know what had happened and how he was doing. Dear God, I prayed.

When I arrived, I was led to a room to await the doctors, and my youngest son came soon after me. The two of us had tears in our eyes, but neither of us knew what to do or say as we sat waiting for someone with information. It wasn't long before a doctor appeared and explained that my oldest son, Steven, had been airlifted from an automobile accident because his heart was not beating when the paramedics arrived at the scene, but they did get it pumping. They took him to one of the best trauma hospitals in the country, Boston's Brigham and Women's Hospital. However, the doctor told us that it stopped again when he was brought in, and they managed to get it going, but they had to put him on machines to keep it pumping. They also put him through a procedure where they brought his body temperature down slowly and would bring it back up slowly over the course of twenty-four hours. They hoped that he would possibly, (but not probably) wake up. Another doctor soon entered the room and added that, because they did not know how long his heart had stopped before the paramedics got there, there was very little chance that he had enough oxygen flowing to his brain to keep him from suffering severe brain damage. My son Michael and I looked at each other with disbelief, fear, and devastation. I only remember screaming, "No, no, no!" and stomping my feet on the floor.

My son Nicholas and his wife, Allison; my two daughters, Colby and Kim; and Kim's husband, Nicholas, flew in from California that same day to be with their brother as we waited to see if a miracle would happen. We all gathered around Steve, praying and witnessing his lifeless body hooked up to machines and covered in metallic blankets. That day felt like an eternity. Family began to fill the waiting room, and food and coffee arrived, but I couldn't even tell you who was there.

Not much changed that day as we sat with Steve. His condition remained the same hour after hour. Very early in the morning of the next day, we were called into a meeting with the doctors to discuss the possibility of taking him off the machines, as they had begun to raise his body temperature and no changes were apparent. I will always remember that meeting, the room, the people, the pacing. I myself could not make a decision and was beyond drained and exhausted, so I suggested we go home to sleep a few hours and return as early as possible to decide what to do. Everyone agreed, and off we went.

We didn't even make it home before the hospital called to tell us that his heart had stopped again. They were able to bring back his heartbeat, but they suggested we come back immediately. We turned around to deal with the final goodbyes and the nightmare of this family crisis. The pain and sadness of this bereavement was unbearable.

That unforgettable day was a nightmare… Our Steven Jr. was gone, his father Steven Sr. had gone twenty-three years earlier, and the shock was immeasurable. The grief and disbelief were overwhelming as we left the hospital in the wee hours of the morning. We all slept a few hours but made sure to make plans to meet that afternoon at our family home and go together to the funeral home, to make arrangements for Steven Jr's burial. I thank God when I think of that day and the way that my adult children, all four of them, and their spouses helped Steve's wife, Leanne, and I make decision after decision. As horrifying as this was, the love of the family was stronger than ever, and it created an energy that made it all possible to manage. In the face of the overwhelming grief was a feeling of pride that this family was again withstanding the unthinkable and doing it with unwavering love and compassion for each other.

Well, the story doesn't end there—oh no, no, no. After we arrived home from the funeral home, my Mother and brothers and sisters were in our house, greeting guests who were offering their condolences. Then, at around eight thirty that evening, three men from the FBI showed up to inform us that, on the same day that Steven Jr. had passed, his father Steven Sr.'s remains had been exhumed from behind a building in Providence, Rhode Island. The very day that our Steven Jr. had passed, his father's remains had been found—not the day before, not the day after, but the very same day. I couldn't make this story up.

Once the FBI had tied up the business at hand and left, my son Michael said to all of us, "I've waited twenty-three years for those men to walk into this house." The energy in the room changed, and we all knew in our hearts that Steven Jr. had to be part of this coincidence. The mystery was solved, and closure was eminent. The day following Steve Jr.'s passing, while meditating, I clearly had a vision of the word *orchestrated* shaped like a rainbow, yes Steven Jr. had orchestrated the discovery of his father's remains. Of all the children, Steven had been the most troubled, over the years, with the unsolved mystery of his father's disappearance. He was the oldest boy and he just couldn't let this difficulty go. He was haunted by the whodunit until his dying day.

Starting on May 9th, 2018, we spent over four months in Boston's Supreme Courthouse for the trial of Steven Sr.'s assassins and his murder. I was the first witness, as his actual disappearance had to be established through my testimony. The facts that followed and the story told were more gruesome and brutal than I could imagine or bear. As a mother, I felt debilitating pain and regret that my children had to hear and see this atrocity played out. The girls flew back and forth from California whenever possible to sit in the courthouse and get the facts as the story was told. However, the boys, Nicholas and Michael, never missed a day. Day after day, they sat, and in the end, they were thankful for the story and the closure. We were all there in the court room, my girls and my boys, when the verdict came in and the assassins were found guilty.

We were able to bury Steven Sr. with his son Steven Jr. and put to rest the years of heartache and perplexity. My children had never made me prouder, and I'm sure their father was impressed by his family's constitution in the face of unfathomable circumstances and losses.

Not a day goes by that I don't think about Steven Sr. and Steven Jr. I don't labor over how, what, where, or why. My story is that they are together and, in a place, more beautiful than we can imagine. I know I'll be with them again someday and everything happens exactly the way it's supposed to in the Divine Plan of creation. I now have angels with me most days who leave little signs and omens. Yes, life moves on, and through it all, you will hopefully come to REALeyes, It's All Good.

As Victor Hugo wrote, "He sought to transform the grief that looks down into the grave by showing it the grief that looks up to the stars."

And in the words of Ralph Waldo Emerson, "Sorrow makes us all children again—destroys all differences of intellect. The wisest know nothing."

Printed in the United States
By Bookmasters